TOM STOPPARD: THE ARTIST AS CRITIC

Tom Stoppard: The Artist as Critic

Neil Sammells

St. Martin's Press   New York

First published in the United States of America in 1988

Printed in Hong Kong

ISBN 0–312–60534–2

Library of Congress Cataloging-in-Publication Data
Sammells, Neil.
Tom Stoppard, the artist as critic.
Bibliography: p.
Includes index.
1. Stoppard, Tom—Criticism and interpretation.
I. Title.
PR6069.T6Z87 1988   822'.914   87–4270
ISBN 0–312–00534–2

For Barbara
and for my parents

Contents

Acknowledgements

I should like to thank the editors of *Critical Quarterly, Modern Drama*, the *Swansea Review* and *The Art of Listening* for permission to use material which had already appeared in different forms. I am grateful to Tom Stoppard himself for answering my enquiries and allowing me to use quotations from his letters. This book was completed with the aid of a research grant from Bath College of Higher Education.

Extracts from the plays *Rosencrantz and Guildenstern Are Dead, Artist Descending a Staircase, After Magritte, The Real Inspector Hound, Travesties, Albert's Bridge, If You're Glad I'll be Frank, Every Good Boy Deserves Favour, Professional Foul* and *Night and Day* are reprinted by permission of Faber and Faber Ltd, London and Grove Press, Inc, New York; extracts from *The Real Thing* are reprinted by permission of Faber and Faber, Inc, London and Boston; and extracts from *Another Moon Called Earth, A Separate Peace, Dogg's Hamlet, Cahoot's Macbeth, The Real Thing, Squaring the Circle, Lord Malquist and Mr Moon*, and *Jumpers* are reprinted by permission of Faber and Faber Ltd, London.

Preface

In *The Real Thing* Henry ('one of your intellectual playwrights') muses on the fate he feels he shares with all artists in general and Elvis Presley in particular: people saying they prefer the earlier stuff. His daughter responds with the not wholly consoling suggestion that maybe he was better then. Stoppard offers this distinction between his own earlier and more recent work in a characteristic spirit of self-mockery and self-protection – but it is my contention that (in respect of the full-length stage-plays at least) the chronological division holds good. The break which separates *Rosencrantz and Guildenstern are Dead, Jumpers* and *Travesties* from *Night and Day* and *The Real Thing* is clear and damaging. Stoppard shifts from applying an aesthetics of engagement to placing his work at the service of a politics of disengagement. I shall not hazard a guess as to whether the same could be said of Elvis Presley.

The structure of my argument is reflected in the two-phase movement of this book. Part I claims that the successful Stoppard is the artist as critic. It contains the first extended discussion of Stoppard's work as a theatre critic for the short-lived magazine *Scene* in the early 1960s and argues that he there sketches out an aesthetics of engagement, the basic premise of which is that artistic freedom cannot exist in a vacuum. Instead, the artist's freedom is seen as a function of his critical engagement with the literary forms at his disposal, an engagement which enables a concomitant critical response on the part of his audience. Part I begins with an examination of Russian Formalist critical theory, based on my notion that its categories and terminology illuminate Stoppard's critical premises and their relationship to his fictional and dramatic practice. (We might almost apply to Stoppard what Boris Eichenbaum says of O. Henry: that it is as if he had taken up 'The Formal Method' and had his ear bent by Viktor Shklovsky.) I then consider Stoppard's drama as a Theatre of Formalism and analyse the different ways in which his work undertakes its critical enterprise.

This critical impulse is defined in the pointed underscoring of generic devices which defines Stoppard's parodic strategies and in his interpretive and transforming 'play' with specific pre-texts such as *Hamlet* and *The Importance of Being Earnest*. I do not, however, attempt a comprehensive survey of the pervading allusiveness of Stoppard's work, though for reasons which will become apparent *Jumpers* and *Travesties* receive a more detailed treatment in this respect. Nor is this book a 'source-study'. The literary bloodline of *The Real Inspector Hound*, for instance, can be traced back beyond Sheridan and Buckingham at least as far as *The Knight of the Burning Pestle* and the inductions of Jonson and Marston; an examination of this relationship would be more at home in a general history of self-consciousness in the English Theatre. Similarly, to attempt an inventory of the literary antecedents of the whodunnit-form of *Jumpers* would have been to consign myself to a series of almost infinite regressions. Instead, I concentrate on only those instances where the 'source' is specific and acknowledged, as in the case of *Travesties* and Wilde, and where Stoppard mounts a thoroughgoing, critical engagement with the pre-text. Considerations of consistency do not, however, prevent me from dwelling on a specific but unacknowledged 'source' for *Rosencrantz and Guildenstern are Dead*: James Saunders' *Next Time I'll Sing to You*.

Part I demonstrates that Stoppard's best work earns its liberty by virtue of its form. In Part II I investigate the political dimension to Stoppard's preoccupation with the nature of freedom and criticism. I stress the continuity between the earlier stuff and recent plays by noting the development of dissenting, peripheral figures into dissidents, but the main thrust of this second part of the argument is to show how Stoppard's work hardens into a militant conservatism that it is both aesthetic and political and which denies his distinctive achievements as a dramatist.

Given the fact that my concern is with mapping out and following a theoretical approach which might best throw into relief both the strengths and weaknesses of Stoppard's work, I have not felt obliged to deal with each of his plays in turn. Consequently, a number of the 'nuts 'n bolts' comedies such as *Dirty Linen* and *The Dog It Was That Died* are not examined here. Stoppard's adaptations from Schnitzler, Nestroy and Molnár are also excluded (although some lessons might have been drawn from the rather desperate facetiousness of *On The Razzle* and *Rough Crossing*). However, *Tango* (adapted from Mrozek) is important to the argument of Part II and I have included it accordingly, preferring again to be inconsistent rather than determinedly neat.

In conclusion, I should like once more to thank Tom Stoppard for permission to quote from his letters to me. No doubt there is much here with which he will disagree, but I hope that he finds my reasons for preferring some of his works to others at least worth engaging with, if not directly relevant to his experience of writing them. I am also grateful for their advice and encouragement to former colleagues at the University of Newcastle upon Tyne, particularly Kelsey Thornton and Bob White, and present colleagues at Bath College of Higher Education (especially Ian Burton, who knows more about self-consciousness than most). My greatest debt is to Barbara, who had no time for typing or proof-reading and prefers my earlier work.

Neil Sammells

Part I

1
Formalism: An Aesthetics
of Engagement

In *The Prison House of Language*, Frederic Jameson suggests that the representative Russian Formalist is the novelist Viktor Shklovsky, the Artist as Critic. An ultimate evaluation of Russian Formalism as a concrete literary phenomen will, he claims, 'bring it much closer to genuinely creative movements such as German Romanticism and Surrealism than to a purely critical doctrine like that of the American New Criticism.'[1] It is a valuable insight. At the heart of Formalist thinking is a thoroughgoing recognition of criticism as creation. A broad-based discussion of the central tenets, and implications, of the Russian Formalist outlook will serve as a first step towards an understanding of the Artist as Critic, and the consistency of an imagination in which Formalist criticism issues in Formalist drama.

As a historical phenomenon, Formalism has its roots in the burst of artistic experimentation and critical iconoclasm which marks the years of the Russian Revolution. It can, perhaps, best be approached through its opponents. For Trotsky, Formalism displayed an abortive idealism applied to questions of art: the nature of its critique of literature and literary tradition was, in the context of a nascent revolution's struggle for survival, fundamentally irresponsible. By concentrating on the problem of form at the apparent expense of content, the Formalists stood accused of decadence. Formalism seemed divorced from the tough practicalities of a world defined by action. 'They believe,' claimed Trotsky of its proponents, 'that in the beginning was the word. But we believe that in the beginning was the deed. The word followed, as its phonetic shadow.'[2] At best intellectually effete, at worst reactionary, Formalism became an enemy of the Revolution. In the wake of the bolshevik victory and consolidation of power, as the logic of history became yoked to the Leninist purpose, Formalism assumed the character of a persecuted sect, many of its adherents being forced into compromise and recan-

tation. It was crushed by the vigour of orthodoxy, a state-promul-
gated poetics dominated by 'reflection theory' which focused on the
degree to which texts revealed the underlying logic of historical
event, the hidden pattern in the red carpet. By the early thirties
Russian Formalism was effectively dead, stifled by Socialist Realism
and Zhdanov, its energetic champion.[3]

In fact, the Russian Formalists were concerned with a fundamental
practicality: the practicality of criticism. Shklovsky and his fellows
believed form worthy of study because they recognised the way it
could exercise furtive control over our ways of seeing, of thinking,
of feeling, of expressing. Value was attributed to that work which
attempted to break the suffocating grip of established form, which,
by making form itself content, held it up for scrutiny and criticism.
To refuse to criticise form (to pay no attention to the procedures of
established literary types) was to accept it as immutable and natural,
as beyond change. For the Russian Formalists such acquiescence was
true artistic irresponsibility and decadence, a chaining of the creative
act to the assumptions of what had already been said. For Trotsky,
'formalism' became a term of disparagement because such concerns,
he believed, issued in an undue preoccupation with the minutiae of
literary forms at the expense of larger considerations. It is Susan
Sontag, heir to the Formalist tradition, who provides the best riposte
to such strictures. As a term of abuse, she says, 'formalism' should
be reserved for those works of art 'which mechanically perpetuate
outmoded or depleted aesthetic formulas [sic].'[4] This is crucial: for
the Russian Formalists the problem of form and its criticism was the
problem of renewal.

By focusing on form the Formalists believed they were uncovering
not the essence, but the distinctive *function* of literary expression.
For Shklovsky and the *Opoyaz* Formalists, literature was not (as it
it was later to be for Roman Jakobson and his fellow Czech Structur-
alists) a system *like* language, but a work *on* language, a critical
reworking of the processes of ordinary discourse. Literariness was
not, as the proponents of 'reflection theory' would have it, an ultimate value possessed by a text (for example, the accuracy and conviction with which it inculcated right-doing by laying bare the inexorable
workings of history) but, rather, a relationship – the relationship it
enjoyed with those non-literary texts which did not perform a distinctive, critical operation on ordinary language. Form came to be
regarded not as something separable from content, but as an activity
which defined the text itself. For Boris Eichenbaum, a new concept

of form had come into play: 'not just the outer covering but the whole entity, something concrete and dynamic, substantive in itself, and unqualified by any correlation.' This signalled, he continues, a departure not only from the transcendentalism of the Symbolists (for whom form was the door to a hidden world) but also from 'aestheticism', 'a delectation with certain elements of form consciously divorced from "content" '.[5] In its initial period of development, the 'Formal Method' (as Eichenbaum calls it) was engaged in a vital and vigorous polemical debate – defining its terms, turning them back against its enemies, arguing for the right to examine its own object of study in its own way.

Central to that study of 'literariness' was the concept of *ostranenie*, or 'making strange'. It is Shklovsky who gives the most graphic description of that process of habituation against which the creative artist must strive. 'The fate of the works of bygone artists of the word,' he tells us, 'is the same as the fate of the word itself . . . both become coated with the glass armour of the familiar.'[6] Literariness is the ability to crack that armour, the protective shell whereby experience, and its expression in established literary form, is rendered unchallengeable. Shklovsky's image is precise: it is not only language which becomes coated and opaque, but literature itself. The text which had once been capable of *ostranenie*, of defamiliarising experience, is soon established as a new norm and loses its critical relationship with those texts which had never attempted to crack, or even become aware of, the glass armour of the familiar. *Ostranenie* is a key concept in the poetics of form: it does not describe an enduring quality which a work can be said to possess, it denotes, instead, a function, a critical function, it can be used to fulfil.

Literature distinguishes itself, according to the Russian Formalists, by means of *ostranenie*, its ability to 'make strange' those forms which appear to assert the eternity of the present, strengthening in us 'the feeling that the things and events among which we live are somehow "natural", which is to say permanent.'[7] The importance to the Formalists of *ostranenie* can be seen in the model of literary history and evolution they constructed, a model founded on the compulsively critical activity of the literary text. For Jameson the peculiar usefulness of the concept of *ostranenie* is that it describes a process 'valid for all literature without in any way implying the primacy of one particular element (such as metaphor) or one particular genre over the others.'[8] In this sense Formalism is the direct antithesis of critical naturalism. Zola, most voluble of the

French Naturalists, asserted literary history as teleology: literature had evolved towards a higher complexity, striving to attain direct observation, exact anatomy, the acceptance and depicting of 'what is'. Writing could thus be evaluated according to the degree to which it approximated and contributed to this Naturalist ideal. 'One thing is certain,' cries Zola, 'that each labourer is working towards the definite triumph of naturalism, even those who appear to fight against it. They are, in spite of everything, borne along by the current of the time.'[9] Nothing, for the Formalists, could be less certain. In the first place, they were vehemently opposed to the idea that any one style of writing could claim to transpose the real from the plane of the actual to that of the verbal. Secondly, the Formalists viewed literary evolution not as progress towards a transparently 'real' way of writing but as the constant reorganisation and regrouping of permanent elements, as the unfolding of a self-generating and self-enclosed sequence of styles and genres. Literary change was not conditioned by any great current in the human mind, as Zola claimed, nor by the social and historical factors of which, Trotsky believed, the word was but a phonetic shadow. The arc of literary change is the arc of criticism: literary evolution is scored by the engagement of Form with Form. '*New form*' explains Shklovsky, '*comes about not in order to express new content but in order to replace an old form that has already lost its artistic viability.*'[10]

For the Formalists, literature is compulsively deforming: to write is not to accept and depict what is, but to deform it. Once the literary work no longer admits the nature and extent of the deformation it enacts and offers itself as a transparent window on the real, it becomes itself the subject of criticism, and deformation. Thus literary history is the struggle of literature to retain consciousness of self, to display the knowledge that as an activity it is essentially critical, and parodic. Indeed, the parodic impulse is identified with the creative impulse. The work which strives to be new does so in terms of a recognition of the failures of its predecessors. Shklovsky again: 'Creation as a parallel with and contrast to some model is a description applicable not just to parody but to any work of art in general.'[11]

This struggle to self-consciousness manifests itself in a variety of ways, as the work attempts to 'foreground' the act of expression. The technique of 'laying bare the device' was, for the Formalists, a favourite example of how literature could use parody to renew its self-consciousness and, hence, its power to make reading a 'strange' experience. Here the propensity for new styles of writing to 'take off' from a critical engagement with the old is quite clearly seen. Erlich, the pioneering historian of the Formalist movement, says that this aspect of *ostranenie* is evident when 'the obsolete device is not thrown overboard, but repeated in a new, incongruous context and thus . . . made "perceptible" again'.[12] This is an extraordinarily fertile suggestion about the nature of that literature which is proud to display its parodic roots. Perhaps no work repeats an obsolete device in a more incongruous context than Samuel Beckett's *Play*, in which the eternal triangle and hackneyed rhetoric of domestic melodrama are relived by three characters immersed in urns, blinded and thrust into sporadic speech by a probing, unnameable light.

Parody is a recognition within the work of literature that the world it must engage is the world as reduced to the structures and procedures of writing, the world as form. Such a recognition is also an awareness of intertextuality, the relationship the text must assume with other acts of writing. David Lodge gives the most succinct definition of intertextuality when he says that no book has any meaning on its own: 'The meaning of a book is in a large part a product of its differences from and similarities to other books. If a novel did not bear some resemblance to other novels we should not know how to read it, and if it wasn't different from all other novels we shouldn't *want* to read it.'[13] To lay bare the devices of other works is one way of asserting difference and of demonstrating self-consciousness. Another way is to follow the law propounded by Shklovsky, the 'canonisation of the junior branch'. To canonise the junior branch is to renew the critical and defamiliarising function of literature by using the devices of sub-literary genres. The Formalists, for instance, were particulary interested in Dostoievsky's employment of whodunnit-motifs in *The Brothers Karamazov*. Dostoievsky, according to Shklovsky, raised the devices of the 'dime novel' to the level of the literary norm. In so doing, Dostoievsky called into question the supposition of superiority inherent in what had previously been considered 'quality' literature. *The Brothers Karamazov* ensures that straightforwardly fine writing, canonised by literary tradition, is made to look bankrupt.

For the Formalists, then, literary evolution was far more complex than had been envisaged by the French Naturalists. The model was defined not by progress, but by mutation. In his study of Gogol and Dostoievsky, Tynyanov claimed that each 'instance of literary succession is first and foremost a struggle involving the destruction of the old unity and a new construction out of the old elements'.[14]

This is a crucial Formalist insight. In denying that literary evolution is simply a matter of continuing on a straight line, Tynyanov emphasises not only the critical dimension to creation and the emergence of a new style, but also the reduction from unity to disorder which this entails. By canonising the junior branch the writer upends the hierarchy of writing in which 'literature' is distinguished from, say, pulp fiction. The upending of order is also perceptible in the individual work. To lay bare a device (the defamiliarising technique of *obnaženie priëma*) is to call attention to the principle of organisation within the text, to the foundation of the world it is attempting to create. The solidity of that world could be called into question by what Fortunatov calls 'negative form'. Frequently employed in the short story, 'negative form' is a sort of literary short-circuit. The story seems to move serenely to a moment of closure which will make sense of, *order*, all that has preceded it. It never occurs. The action remains incomplete. The reader is left with a familiar narrative pattern made strange by its incompleteness. (Jameson notes that 'negative form' is a particularly useful critical tool to apply to the stories of de Maupassant.[15]) For Jakobson, this disordering attack on both literary tradition and the literary work was largely a question of critical engagement with 'the dominant'.

The dominant is defined by Jakobson as the focusing component of a work of art, ruling, determining and transforming the remaining components. To shift the dominant, to elevate a component from the position of ordered to ordering, is to destroy the integrity of a style or genre, challenging its claims to present a world both natural and permanent. For the Formalist, then, creation is a power-struggle. It is an expression of dissatisfaction on the part of the artist, an attempt to refuse the dictates of hierarchy.

We are here at the crux of the Formalist position: the recognition of the interplay of freedom and necessity which characterises the activity of the artist. To register his dissatisfaction, to restore to the text the power of the word to surprise and liberate us, the artist must engage the hierarchy of literature, but can never free himself from that domain. Literature remains a closed field of techniques which can be parodied, demoted, mocked, or put to strange and unheard of uses – but they can never be entirely dispensed with, only pushed into the background from which, one day, they will re-emerge, honed and dangerous, their cutting-edge restored. ' "Creative freedom" ', claims Tynyanov, 'thus becomes an optimistic slogan which does not correspond to reality, but yields instead to the slogan "creative necessity" '.[16] Part of that necessity is the artist's responsibility to his reader or audience: *ostranenie* is, after all, merely a function of the relationship between work and reader, the degree to which the former awakens a critical response in the latter. The reader, according to Jakobson, 'has a vivid awareness of two orders: the traditional canon and the artistic novelty as a deviation from that canon. It is precisely against the background of that tradition that innovation is conceived. The Formalist studies brought to light that this simultaneous preservation of tradition and breaking away from tradition form the essence of every new work of art.'[17] Creative necessity demands that both aspects are perceptible; it is an exacting task, demanding of the artist a fine sensitivity towards both tradition and innovation.

In *The Prison House of Language* Frederic Jameson makes a useful comparison between the Formalists' conception of *ostranenie* and Brecht's *Verfremdungseffekt*. Both *ostranenie* and *Verfremdungseffekt* are conceived as correctives to habituation. Significantly, Brecht shares the Formalists' insistence that no single, discoverable literary technique could be regarded as capable of performing this function under all or any circumstances. 'So,' asks Brecht about his Epic Theatre, 'is this new style of production *the* new style; is it a complete and comprehensive technique, the final result of every experiment? Answer: no. It is *a* way, the one that *we* have followed.'[18] According to Jameson the purpose of this struggle is 'a political one in the most thoroughgoing sense of the word; it is, as Brecht insists over and over, to make you aware that the objects and institutions you thought to be natural were really only historical: the result of change, they themselves henceforth become in their turn changeable.'[19] In fact, Brecht's emphasis on the inevitably political implications of a shaking of the audience's sense of the structure of their world was foreshadowed by a number of contemporaries of those Formalists like Shklovsky who claimed that the act of defamiliarisation was essentially 'unmotivated': a response only to the literary circumstances in which the writer found himself. The Futurists, led by Mayakovsky and Khlebnikov, were revolutionaries in both art and politics, men who, as the title of their manifesto of 1912 suggests, were dedicated to delivering *A Slap In The Face Of Public Taste*.

For the Futurists art was an inescapably political activity, a means of liberating consciousness from the shackles of the past. Mayakovsky's participation in the activities of the Moscow Linguistic Circle and of *Opoyaz*, the two seed-beds of Formalism, ensured an exchange of ideas between the two movements. In the hands of the Futurists the Formalists' preoccupation with the functions and the possibilities of the literary device assumed an overt political colouring: a particular way of writing lost its artistic viability when, by becoming part of the literary norm and assuming its allotted place in the scheme of what was, it no longer prompted the reader to a consideration of what might be. Thus the Futurists demonstrated the politics of art by attacking the Russian Lyric with their own transsense, non-sense *zaum* poetry. Mayakovsky shouted his fractured lines in a yellow blazer with blue roses painted on his cheeks, and was, as Tom Stoppard tells us in *Travesties*, damned by Lenin for so doing. In fact, Mayakovsky provides a historical as well as a theoretical link between Formalism and Brecht. The playwright first used the term 'verfremden' after seeing the Chinese actor Mei Lan-Fang at a private performance arranged in Moscow by Mayakovsky's friend and supporter, Sergei Tretiakov. Bernhard Reich recalls that he first heard 'verfremden' used by Tretiakov in Brecht's presence and concludes that he adopted the formulation as a description first of the Chinese methods and then of his own.[20]

In rehabilitating Formalist thinking after its suppression within Russia, Roland Barthes has consistently emphasised its potentially political implications; in so doing he has elaborated upon Formalist insights into the nature of the way we read. For Barthes, as for the Futurists, a particular style of writing is irredeemably part of the political power-structure in which it is practised. He uses the term *écriture* to describe writing which although developed under particular historical circumstances for specific political ends, is intent on protesting its own innocence. Barthes is equally insistent that in reading and writing there is no such thing as innocence. Just as no text can claim to be innocent of a peculiar deformation (or encoding) of the world it purports to represent, so the reader brings to the text a range of suppositions about that world, his place in it, and the way art should reflect it. A text can be evaluated by the extent to which it reinforces this sense of security and permanence. Again Barthes provides a useful terminology to describe what is, for him, a qualitative difference. The *écrivant* produces writing which is tailor-made for the reading-habits of his public. The *écrivain*, on the other hand, manages, by some means or other, to 'alienate' his reader. The *écrivant* treats the reader as a passive consumer, proffering a meaning to which the reader is slowly, but beguilingly, led. The *écrivain*, however, produces a book about nothing but itself, calling attention to its own status as pure style.

The particular political affiliations of Barthes are here quite conspicuous: the writing he denigrates is that which sponsors an exchange analogous to the cash-nexus characterising capitalism. Like the Formalists he espouses the work which criticises, and which awakens a critical response in the reader: alienated from writing once taken on trust, he begins to examine that world embodied within it. In his later work Barthes moves away from his preoccupation with writing which is specifically critical of the capitalist *écriture* and concentrates, instead, on the broader implications of the critical operations of the valued text. He advocates the *texte de jouissance*, which offers to the reader not the pleasure of discovering a unitary meaning, but the copulative, orgasmic bliss of savouring its linguistic surface. A precondition of this intercourse between work and reader is the very absence within the text of that order which makes the communication of *meaning* possible. The *texte de jouissance* is, in this sense, an array of devices or components without an ordering, structuring dominant. The reader has to engage in a thoroughly critical activity, consciously producing a variety of provisional 'meanings' within the work. In *S/Z* Barthes rapes a Realist text: he reduces Balzac's *Sarrasine* to a disordered confusion of signifying movements, of literary tricks. Classical Realism, the window on the world, emerges as a dense and duplicitous medium. *S/Z* turns the *readerly* text of the *écrivant* into the *writerly* text of Barthes the critic.

Barthes's work is valuable for the critical tools it gives us to explore the nature of reading and the reader, for following through the implications of the Russian Formalists' discussion of art as strategy – and less so for his re-enactment of the relationship between work and reader as psycho-sexual melodrama. At root, Barthes's critical categories elaborate upon a basic opposition suggested by Shklovsky: between 'seeing' and 'recognising'. Shklovsky claims that we do not experience the familiar, 'we do not see it, we recognise it'. He adds, with a Proustian eye for the significance of domestic detail, we 'do not see the walls of our rooms'.[21] Roman Jakobson, in his withering attack on the pretensions of realism in art, says that the task of the artist-innovator (Barthes's *écrivain*) is to impose a new form upon our perception, 'if we are to detect in a given thing those traits which went unnoticed the day before'.[22]

Jakobson's later work with the Prague School represents, in fact, a fascinating refinement of the central Russian Formalist tenets. Literature is now seen as a system fundamentally similar to language: both represent closed fields of limiting possibilities. The character of language, claims Jakobson, is fundamentally twofold: speech is defined by the twin operations of selection and combination. These two modes (or poles) Jakobson called the *metaphoric* (governing selection) and the *metonymic* (governing combination). The crux of Jakobson's argument was reached in his treatment and observation of aphasics, who, he noted, fell into two classes: those who had difficulty selecting the correct word from any apposite paradigm, and those who could not combine their choices into meaningful utterances. In each case one of the fundamental operative processes of language had been blocked. Paradoxically, the aphasic can be seen as the archetypal language-user: although, in normal verbal behaviour, both processes are continually operative 'careful observation will reveal that under the influence of a cultural pattern, personality, and verbal style, preference is given to one of the two processes over the other'.[23] This is indeed a closed field: language is reduced to two modes of operation and, at any one time, the language-user (and this includes the artist as well as the ordinary speaker) is constrained to employ one at the expense of the other, to aspire, so to speak, to a condition of aphasia.

David Lodge has applied Jakobson's insights both to concrete critical tasks in particular, and to the problem of literary change in general. For Lodge, the modern artist is in continual rebellion against the poverty of his expressive material. This rebellion imparts a cyclical rhythm to literary history: faced with the preponderance of one of the two operative modes, the writer tries to resuscitate language by turning to the other. Realism, which is essentially metonymic because dedicated to combining elements in logical sequence and placing them in a recognisable context, is superseded by its opposite: writing which, by operating metaphorically, asserts the non-logical similarity between elements rather than the causal links between them. Jakobson's model of language as a closed field provides Lodge with the explanation for 'why innovation is so often a return to the last fashion but one in some respects; why, within the modern period, phases of metaphoric experiment seem to alternate with phases of metonymic realism. If Jakobson is right, there is nowhere for writing to go except between these two poles.'[24] The nature of creativity and revolt is thus defined by the mechanics of language itself.

Lodge's achievement, the measure of the work he has performed *on* Jakobson's Formalism, lies principally in the suggestions he makes about the nature of postmodernist writing. Condemned to a language which can work either metaphorically or metonymically, the postmodernist must struggle to articulate his dissatisfaction with that very tyranny. Postmodernism is, hence, a Poetics of Criticism: the writer's critical analysis of the presence of the two poles is coupled with a critical dismissal of that language embalmed in prevailing literary practice. Our liveliest writers, Lodge tells us, have consciously or intuitively grasped the structural principles of the literary system. A critical analysis of the field of possibilities open to these writers has shown it to be closed indeed: they share the Russian Formalists' sense that literary change is the constant reorganisation and re-grouping of permanent elements. Accepting this constriction in an attempt to transcend it, postmodernists have ganged up to cheat 'Literature'; refusing to choose between a dominantly metaphoric or metonymic mode of writing 'they employ both, in extreme, contradictory, often absurd or parodic ways, within the same work or body of work.'[25]

Samuel Beckett is, as far as Lodge is concerned, the archetypal postmodernist writer. In terms of Jakobson's model, the extreme difficulty of much modern writing can only be caused by a disruption or dislocation of either the selection or the combination axes of language. Of Beckett's work 'it is not an exaggeration to say that it aspires to a condition of aphasia.'[26] In this sense aphasia becomes an act of liberation. It attains its own eloquence. The pendulum of language swings between metaphor and metonymy; Beckett seizes it, speeds the arc to the beat of his will. Yet the mechanism survives.

Lodge's postmodernist is, then, the artist as critic; it might be added that Beckett's status as a representative postmodernist is emphasised by the existence of an independent and important body of work: his critical writings on literature and painting. These pieces (denigrated and disavowed by their author, defended by his admirers) display recognisably Formalist traces. There is at least this to be said for art criticism, claims Beckett, implicitly plotting the limits of his own endeavours, 'that it can dispel from the eyes, before *rigor vitae* sets in, some of the weight of congenital prejudice'.[27] The task he thus sets himself is clear, and echoes an opposition central to Shklovsky: to lift from the eyes the film of recognition and to return the possibility of sight. Throughout his criticism the writers and artists he praises are those whose work itself undertakes the

same task. For the young Beckett, it is Joyce who leads the assault
on glass-armoured prejudice, and the terms in which he describes
Work in Progress (*Finnegans Wake*) are a remarkably accurate antici-
pation of Barthes's distinction between the *écrivain* and the *écrivant*.
In *Work in Progress* form is content and content is form, he declares:
Joyce's writing 'is not *about* something; *it is that something itself*'.[28]
In other words, Joyce is the *écrivain* whose work is, in Barthes's
sense, intransitive and, as such, a deliberate challenge to the
cultured, casual reader. In *Proust* (Beckett's best-known critical
essay) he focuses on the French writer's concern with the conflict
between Voluntary and Involuntary Memory. Voluntary Memory is
seen as a function of habit and Involuntary Memory performs a
critical operation by presenting an alternative version of the past.
This conflict restates, of course, the opposition between habitual,
mechanical performance and its breakdown which is at the very
centre of the Formalist critical model. Proust's achievement is in
integrating this thematic concern with his formal practices, which
Beckett sees as a denial of the habitual procedures of Realism and
Naturalism. O'Casey is similarly praised for the degree to which
he refuses the easy option; the essential O'Casey, we are told, is
distinguished from the incidental O'Casey (the would-be lyric poet
of *Windfalls*) by his use of slapstick or 'knockabout' comedy in
his drama. Again the similarity with Formalist approaches is clear:
O'Casey is seen to be canonising the junior branch.[29] In essence,
then, Beckett insists that the vitality and validity of the creative act
is a function of its critical engagement with old ways of seeing and
of saying, and he coins a phrase to describe that which binds artist
and critic in a unity of response: analytical imagination.[30]

In Beckett's own drama and novels the analytical imagination is
most visibly evident in the prevalence of parody. The importance of
parody in Beckett's work has been noted by several critics but none
has related it specifically to the Formalist preoccupations of his
poetics. We would do well, however, to listen to James Knowlson
and John Pilling and not be misled by Beckett's comment that an
empty theatre constituted more or less ideal conditions for the presentation of his plays: 'Consciousness of an audience's expectations
and needs is implicit in all that Beckett has written for the stage,
whether the presence or independent role of that audience is
acknowledged or not.'[31] Beckett's search for expressive freedom
is defined, then, by his sense of responsibility to his audience, a

responsibility discharged by his parodic engagement with habitual forms eliciting habitual response.

Tom Stoppard is also the artist as critic. As in Beckett's case, the critical impulse is not just a constituent of his creative enterprise, it gives rise to a substantial body of critical writing. Interestingly, Stoppard the critic investigates the degree to which he feels Beckett meets his responsibility to his audience in pursuing new modes of dramatic expression. A detailed examination of Stoppard's criticism will not only shed new light on the relationship between the two playwrights, it will also prepare the ground for a demonstration of the ways in which Stoppard's Theatre of Parody can be seen as the practical application of a Formalist aesthetics of engagement.

2

Stoppard as Critic

I

'There is,' Tom Stoppard claims, 'a sort of second-rate journalism that presents the journalist more than the subject.' He adds, without embarrassment, 'I did that.'[1] From September 1962 to April 1963 Stoppard reviewed the London theatre for the magazine *Scene*. He had completed two plays: *A Walk on the Water* and *The Gamblers*. Neither had been produced professionally on the stage. Many of the reviews he wrote during his time on *Scene* are of no interest, telling us little of the journalist and less of the subject. 'I wasn't much of a critic,' he has told me, pointing out that the pieces suffered all the usual drawbacks of magazine work, being written in haste and cut for space.[2] However, a number of the longer articles have been shamefully neglected by his critics (only Joan Dean's portentously titled *Tom Stoppard: Comedy as a Moral Matrix* makes any significant reference to these early reviews); they shed light on his own work and reveal a developing critical outlook which awaits the consistency and vigour it will attain in his dramatic writings, in which criticism becomes an integral aspect of the creative enterprise, Stoppard's theatre emerging as a battle of the books, a clamorous argument of form with form. Despite his self-deprecation, the best work on *Scene* shows Stoppard's critical powers at full stretch; it illuminates not just the journalist but Stoppard the playwright as well – particularly when his subject is Beckett.

Critics were, of course, quick to point out similarities between Beckett's work and the play which first made Stoppard's name: *Rosencrantz and Guildenstern are Dead*. Ronald Bryden, reviewing the original student production at the 1966 Edinburgh Festival, described the play as an existential fable unabashedly dedicated to *Waiting For Godot* 'but as witty and vaulting as Beckett's original is despairing'. When it opened in London the following spring Bryden noted that the National Theatre production picked out the darker themes which had been obscured by the verbal fireworks of the

16

student version. 'The shortest cut to grasping its quality,' he suggested, 'is to imagine the inspired quartet of *Beyond the Fringe* pushing their Shakespeare parody onto the bleak, metaphysical uplands of Samuel Beckett.' In the *Sunday Times* Harold Hobson identified it as the work of a 'spirit deep, foreboding, and compassionate like Beckett' married to a sleight of hand as cunning as Feydeau's. Other critics, however, found it difficult to rid themselves of the suspicion that Stoppard was merely straining for a seriousness belied by the 'undergraduate joke' that defined the play, as if the National Theatre production, darkening the hues of the original, were aiding his trickery. Philip Hope-Wallace had the sensation that a fairly witty and pithy theatrical joke was being elongated merely to make an evening of it: 'Tedium, even kept at bay, made itself felt.' Robert Brustein, writing in the *New Republic*, was even more damning: Stoppard, he announced, does not fight hard enough for insights which come to him, prefabricated, from other plays. Derivative, familiar and prosaic in execution, *Rosencrantz and Guildenstern are Dead* is described as a theatrical parasite, a form of 'Beckett without tears'.[3]

In fact, the connection between Stoppard and Beckett deserves to be taken seriously. Self-advertised by Stoppard, it is much more than an attempt by the theatre's 'intellectual P. T. Barnum' to gain a degree of spurious intellectual integrity. He is not merely playing Jack Worthing to the critics' Lady Bracknell and diligently following the advice to acquire some artistic relations and at any rate one parent before his season as the West End's most successful commercial playwright is quite over. 'Most people who say Beckett,' Stoppard points out, 'mean *Waiting for Godot*. They haven't read his novels, for example. I can see a lot of Beckettian things in all my work, but they're not actually to do with the image of two lost souls waiting for something to happen, which is why most people connect "Rosencrantz" with *Waiting For Godot*, because they had this scene in common.'[4] Stoppard's two *Scene* articles on Beckett go some way to explaining the significance of this remark and to identifying the 'Beckettian things' which are so characteristic of his own best writing. They suggest that Beckett's importance to Stoppard may be of a different kind from that claimed by even the most laudatory reviewers of *Rosencrantz and Guildenstern are Dead*.

Stoppard's first article on Beckett is a review of *End of Day*, a one-man 'display of Beckettry' at the New Arts Theatre presented by Beckett's friend Jack MacGowran in October 1962. *End of Day* was composed of a series of speeches and scenes from Beckett's work, loosely hung around the skeletal frame of *Act Without Words*. Beckett's characters, claims Stoppard, vacillate in a wasteland between blind hope and dumb despair, 'rebounding back and forth from lifeless capitulation to a short-lived sense of purpose, caught between memory and desire.' This vacillation is a comic spectacle: MacGowran captures the 'comic essence of the Beckett refugee', his eyes alight with 'childish delight' and 'haunted by experience'. Stoppard admits that at first sight there is something arbitrary about this channelling of speeches from eight different sources into one character; but it works 'because Beckett's view of man's estate is consistent in all of them, a look of pity and ironic amusement, the exact opposite of laughing till one cries – crying till one laughs.'[5]

Stoppard is here focusing on the magnetic pull of polarities which he sees as defining the structure of Beckett's work. The individual elements (hope, despair, innocence, experience, pity, amusement) are, he suggests, less important than the shape they create: 'Everything is cancelled out; Beckett (see Martin Esslin's *The Theatre of the Absurd*) is much impressed by St Augustine's words, "Do not despair – one of the thieves was saved. Do not presume – one of the thieves was damned." '[6] Later, Stoppard was to enlarge on this act of cancellation at the centre of Beckett's work, describing it as 'confident statement followed by immediate refutation by the same voice. It's a consistent process of elaborate structure and sudden – and total – dismantlement.'[7] 'I find Beckett deliciously funny,' he confesses, 'in the way that he qualifies everything as he goes along, reduces, refines and dismantles.'[8] These remarks, made by an established playwright assaying an understanding of his own work, are compounded by the early article in *Scene:* 'Nothing happens. Nobody comes. Nobody goes. It's awful. It's so awful you have to laugh. When I saw it, hardly anyone did – they had come for punishment, as a misguided tribute to Beckett. He would not thank them for it'.[9]

The *Scene* review of *End of Day* suggests, then, that Stoppard's later remarks, which insist that his humour is the most important factor in Beckett's influence on his work, are not simply those of the clown who wishes to be taken seriously: a desperate casting around for a respectable intellectual pedigree to justify his own comic successes. It also calls into question the judgement of those reviewers of *Rosencrantz and Guildenstern are Dead* who, faintly embarrassed by the play's comedy, seized eagerly upon the 'Beckettian' resonances of the National Theatre production, associating a deepening and darkening of theme with Beckett's vision of two lost souls waiting for something to happen. As a critic Stoppard expresses an immediate and imaginative grasp of the deeply self-deprecating humour of Beckett's writing – laughter celebrating the principle of collapse. Stoppard's appreciation of Beckett's comic strategies is similar to Pirandello's claim that the task of the humorist is to dispel the assumption of certainty and fixity by asserting the contrary position. Sometimes, notes Pirandello, the humorist may pretend to take only one side of a particular thought, but 'inside, the other feeling speaks out to him, and appears although he doesn't have the courage to reveal it. It speaks to him and starts by advancing now a faint excuse, an alternative, which cools off the warmth of the first feeling, and then a wise reflection which takes away seriousness and leads to laughter.'[10] Stoppard recognises that Beckett's laughter in *End of Day* is the index of his critical endeavours, a cancellation of any response which threatens to become dominant – or habitual.

The second *Scene* article on Beckett is of vital importance for the way it helps to define the points of *divergence* between his work and Stoppard's. Stoppard has said that at the time when *Waiting For Godot* was first done 'it liberated something for anybody writing plays. It redefined the minima of theatrical validity.'[11] What is especially interesting about Stoppard's review of *Happy Days* at the Royal Court is that it clarifies his understanding of those conditions which constitute 'theatrical validity'. The review investigates the relationship between what Tynyanov calls creative freedom and creative necessity. Stoppard balances, with great care, the value of Beckett's act of self-liberation from established procedure against his necessary responsibilities to an audience.

Happy Days, claims Stoppard, is the testing-point of Beckett's independence of stage conventions. The problem, as he sees it, is that the contraction of Beckett's drama has encouraged a uniform shrinking of enterprise among the young playwrights he has influenced. 'The tendency of a decade,' Stoppard had claimed earlier, in pointing out the extent to which Christopher Fry's *Curtmantle* departed from prevailing trends, 'has been towards an ever-narrowing field of vision which has its ultimate in two men locked in a wardrobe.'[12] What his review of *Happy Days* makes clear is Stoppard's awareness of the problematic relationship between the creating artist and those conventions with which he must engage. In *Waiting For Godot*, he notes, Beckett's drama of subtraction had freed the theatre from what he calls elsewhere 'the plot-riddled uproar of domestic crisis'[13] without taking it to the extremes of dramatic inaction envisaged in his remarks about the closet-dialogue: 'In "Godot" the nature of the statement – the human situation – did not snub those conventions so much as preclude them, at the same time as the quality of the statement allowed it to work as *theatre*.'[14] In *Happy Days*, however, it would seem that Beckett has deliberately transgressed the limits of theatrical validity.

There is no very good reason, Stoppard declares, why *Happy Days* should be acted rather than read: 'From the little of "Godot" and the less of *Endgame*, we have reached the least of *Happy Days* and dramatically it is not enough.'[15] This is a telling statement about the nature of Stoppard's own drama. *Happy Days* cancels dramatic action: what it lacks is that sense of 'elaborate structure and sudden – and total – dismantlement'. The presence of elaborate structure (a conscious reapplication rather than snubbing of existing stage conventions) is for Stoppard a precondition of that awareness of two orders, the traditional canon and the artistic novelty as a deviation from that canon, which for Jakobson and his Formalist colleagues is a function of the work's literariness and its powers of *ostranenie*. Beckett's artistic novelty, his act of liberation, has lost the background against which it can be seen.

'The interesting thing about comedy,' remarked Stoppard more recently 'is that it works in two completely different ways. It works by surprising people and by gratifying their expectations.'[16] By arousing their expectations in one direction, comedy can fulfil a critical function by surprising them from another. This is why he finds Beckett 'deliciously funny' and also why, for him, *Happy Days* fails. His most damning remark is that it might as well be read as performed. The play fails to evoke the two orders and to engage with the audience's expectations of the theatrical experience. *Happy Days* lacks, in other words, that sense of a disciplined departure from established procedure which defines the comic and the critical strategies of Stoppard's own best work. The two *Scene* reviews of Beckett's work suggest the true nature of his influence on Stoppard. Stoppard responds to Beckett the artist as critic; he takes the distinctive bent of his humour (the insistent presence of a critical counter-movement which cancels any position or response which promises to become dominant or habitual) and uses it not to advance a statement on the human condition, but as a principle of composition.

Stoppard's review suggests that *Happy Days* shirks the problem of the demands and the possibilities presented to the artist by established styles and genres. Beckett, it is implied, has not fought hard enough for his liberty and has neglected his responsibilities to the audience. What is fascinating about the better articles in *Scene* is that they are directed at uncovering the exact nature of artistic freedom. Repeatedly they reach a distinctively Formalist conclusion in characterising such freedom as the freedom of the critic. A typical case in point is his review of Hugh Wheeler's *Big Fish, Little Fish;* the review is doubly interesting because of the light it sheds on *A Walk on the Water*, the play Stoppard had completed some two years previously and which, after rewriting and several changes of title, became *Enter a Free Man*.

Wheeler's play, Stoppard claims, lays itself open to the suspicion of having been assembled from a tried and tested theatrical cookbook. Much of contemporary American drama, he tells us, is a celebration of the failed tightrope-walker: we discover him firmly established on one secure platform, warily eyeing the other, 'ideals/opportunity/ individuality/ and or moral uplift'. Stoppard notes the influence here of Arthur Miller but points out that lately lesser men have been 'giving frustration a whirl in an alien context: drawing-room comedy spiked with newly acceptable neuroses, guaranteed to flatter the intellect, painlessly'. Wheeler has done a professional job, but Stoppard is adamant that nothing original is being attempted; he proclaims a sense of 'deep, detached familiarity' with the 'unfolding of *Big Fish, Little Fish*'.[17]

The problem is that Wheeler's play has duplicated established form in an uncritical way. In a sense, the form has failed to achieve the status of content: to be examined in its own right. Had Wheeler allowed his tightrope-walker to get across, says Stoppard, the play would have been staggeringly original, though pointless; had he allowed him to return on his own decision, it might have been moving. 'But,' he concludes, 'the outcome is forced on the character extraneously, and the play is therefore merely complete, tidy.'[18] It is an interesting observation. Wheeler has capitulated to the terms within which he is expected to work. The play's tidiness attests to the degree to which the artist has been dictated to, has had procedure forced upon him in the same way as the play's outcome is forced upon its protagonist. By mechanically perpetuating 'outmoded or depleted aesthetic formulas [sic]', *Big Fish, Little Fish* is 'formalist' in Susan Sontag's derogatory sense of the term.

Enter a Free Man is the story of another failed tightrope-walker: the inept dreamer hoping to assert his individuality against the collective ethic by means of his inventions. It is interesting to see Stoppard applauding the reflection of his own preoccupations, at a time when the play was undergoing gestation, in two reviews he wrote for the *Bristol Evening World* in 1960. In the first he claims that Richard Attenborough's film *The Angry Silence* equates the twin ideals of the medium: to entertain and to educate. In so doing it achieves a blend as complete 'as a row of chorus-girls explaining Einstein's theory of light – and just about as rare'.[19] The image, of course, would not be inappropriately applied to the intellectual exuberance of Stoppard's own work such as *Jumpers* and *Travesties*. However, the review sheds light on *Enter a Free Man* by describing the film (the story of a factory-worker's refusal to buckle under union pressure) as 'a cry from the dock on behalf of every stubborn, proud, infuriating little man who has ever committed the crime of preferring to do his own thinking for himself.'[20] The remark emphasises, obliquely, the positive side of George Riley's revolt in *Enter a Free Man* and helps to close the gap between the comic, peripheral figures of Stoppard's early plays and the political dissidents of the later. However, a further dimension to George's plight is suggested by a second film review – of Peter Sellers's *The Battle of the Sexes*, which chronicles the fortunes of a Dickensian firm of Scottish tweed weavers resisting the intrusion of the twentieth century in the form of an American efficiency expert. Sellers, the little man, rebels 'and this is like a rabbit showing its teeth; no matter how ferocious the effect is meant to be, the result is merely comic.'[21]

George's revolt is a mediated one. To use Lucien Goldmann's terminology: he is a classic example of the problematic individual, the dissenter who, in rejecting collective values, is unable to assert in their place a truly independent and authentic set of his own. In effect, his revolt cancels itself; it embodies that principle of contradiction which, for Stoppard, is essentially comic. Ever ready to accuse his pub audience of being controlled by forces outside themselves, George is sublimely unaware of the received nature of his own dreams of famed and lucrative individualism; they are, in fact, simply manifestations of the structures which condition and perpetuate collective, social behaviour. His grandly conceived revolt is nothing of the sort – merely a retreat into the fantasy of his inventions such as indoor rain and the reversible envelope. Riley is Stoppard's dramatisation of a paradox: he demonstrates the need to criticise conventions (in his case social forms and expectations) and yet unwittingly emphasises the impossibility of our ever freeing ourselves completely from them. This paradox defines the dilemma not only of the spiritual loner, the failed tightrope-walker, but also that of the artist faced with the expectations of form and genre: creation is the act of criticising them, not of vainly hoping to dispense with them altogether.

Of *Enter a Free Man* Stoppard says that he feels a great deal of gratitude and affection, and a certain amount of embarrassment: 'It works pretty well as a play, but it's actually phoney because it's a play written about other people's characters.'[22] Its derivative nature has led Stoppard to refer to it as 'Death of a Flowering Salesman', acknowledging the debt to Miller and Robert Bolt. Its literary ancestry does not, of course, stop there: Riley's self-proclaimed status as inventor, and the fostering of his illusions by his family, recall Ibsen's *The Wild Duck*. Stoppard's embarrassment is caused, however, less by his borrowing from other writers (almost ubiquitous in his later work) than by the fact that this acquisition does not in itself become the subject of attention. George's habitual self-dramatisation, his theatrical entrances and stagey rhetoric, does not constitute an elevation of form to the status of content. Like *Big Fish, Little Fish* the play pays respect to form and obediently follows procedure, emerging as a triumph of the tidy mind. When *Enter a Free Man* opened in London in 1968 – some five years after being broadcast as a television play – it caused a certain amount of unrest among reviewers. J. W. Lambert felt that, tactically, Stoppard had made a mistake in refurbishing it for the stage: 'it will certainly release damaging waves of reaction against the enormous success of "Rosencrantz and Guildenstern".' Philip Hope-Wallace found it 'nice and kindly but rather dull', while the most considered objections came from Irving Wardle in *The Times*. The main virtues of the play, he claimed, were its theatrical neatness and the chance it gave Michael Hordern as George to steal the show. It did not, however, suggest a strong individual talent: 'What this proves, I think, is the power of theatrical convention to take over from the playwright.' In other words, Wardle criticises Stoppard in much the same terms as the latter had criticised Wheeler. *Enter a Free Man* was a professional job producing 'a depressing sense of facility',[23] an accusation which recalls Stoppard's 'deep, detached familiarity' with *Big Fish, Little Fish*.

Stoppard's experience with *Big Fish, Little Fish* seems to have been repeated many times during his visits to the London theatre. 'There is something about the current writing scene,' he claimed, bewailing the ascendancy of the tried-and-tested theatrical cookbook from which Wheeler had gleaned his recipe, 'which encourages this sort of analysis, suggesting a given number of dramatic idioms to be used in any combination, like a Readymix which leaves the cook to add corn or break in a fresh egghead according to taste.'[24] He dismisses such plays-from-the-packet as 'not so much written as typed'.[25] He dramatises himself as a man haunted by clichés and stereotypes,'waiting for a Catholic priest who isn't Irish'.[26] In 'Who Killed Peter Saunders?' Stoppard takes this self-dramatisation a step further. The article takes the form of a brief playlet on the subject of the plethora of thrillers in the West End and is an early example of that fascination with stereotypes which is so insistent in, for example, *Travesties*. It is doubly interesting inasmuch as it is something of an embryonic *The Real Inspector Hound*, presenting, as it does, a critic who becomes caught up in the play he is reviewing.

The critic in question is one Slurp who is typing suavely on his custom-built 'Louis Quinze' Olivetti, smoking Russian cigarettes and wearing a dressing-gown autographed by Noel Coward. He notes that Agatha Christie's *The Mousetrap* seems to have stumbled on the key to perpetual motion and that the past two months have seen London productions of seven other 'whodunnits'. He quotes the opinions of Peter Saunders, who is the producer of Christie's *Rule of Three* at the Duchess and who denies that thrillers and suchlike depend on a manipulation which has no literary quality but which allows, and indeed encourages, cardboard characters: ' "the press keeps calling them cardboard characters, but I prefer to call them larger than life. In the theatre there is room for everybody, surely." Well said, Mr Saunders, I say.' At this point Slurp is interrupted by D.I. Rafferty and P.C. Wilkins, who 'appear to be made out of cardboard' and who ask him if he is the author of 'Whodunnits Cluttering Up Social Theatre' and 'Complacent Escapism An Insult To My Intelligence'. Slurp admits that he is and Rafferty tells him that Peter Saunders is dead. 'Good God, who murdered him?' cries Slurp, springing the trap. 'Who said anything about murder?' asks Rafferty. 'Well . . . I thought . . . I assumed it was one of those plays,' mumbles Slurp. Saunders, we learn, has been struck down in his library with the quarto hide-bound edition of Christie's works. 'You'll never get me alive,' he announces, dropping dead. Cardboard Constable Wilkins has the last word: 'He was right – it *is* one of those plays.'[27]

In reviewing *The Real Inspector Hound* Irving Wardle touched on a central strategy which the play shares with 'Who Killed Peter Saunders?'. He claims that Moon and Birdboot, the two critics who become entangled in the action of the play they are reviewing, are as unreal as the characters in the thriller; there is no difference, he contends, between their private feelings and their parodied critical pronouncements. Having put the critics on stage, Stoppard completes the equation of artifice by installing two of the actors in the critics' seats. This kind of thing, continues Wardle, happens regularly in Stoppard's plays: 'He establishes different planes of action, and then negates the contrast by showing up every plane as equally unreal. His work is a series of looking-glass adventures; with the difference that his mirrors reflect nothing but themselves. There is no starting-point in actuality.' This makes his work fatuously inhuman: 'His comedy is like the grin of a Cheshire cat; disembodied and as remote from the ordinary human passions as pure mathematics.'[28] In many ways Wardle's criticism is an extension of his earlier disparaging remarks about *Enter a Free Man*. Peopled by theatrical automata, that play was simply a demonstration of mechanistic artifice, a reflection of conventional theatrical experience. His review of *The Real Inspector Hound* is a slight change in the angle of attack: he now acknowledges that Stoppard is *deliberately* reflecting theatrical experience, and that part of this undertaking is a preoccupation with his own procedures. The looking-glass adventure which unfolds in 'Who Killed Peter Saunders?' is of exactly that type described by Wardle. The contrast between the critic and his subject – the world of the 'whodunnits' and the cardboard policemen – is negated; each is shown to be equally unreal. Everything, in effect, is cancelled out. The apparently dominant plane of action is criticised by a counter-movement. Comic contradiction is the principle of composition.

Criticism like Wardle's has confronted Stoppard throughout his career. His response has been trenchant. 'I think that sort of truth-telling writing', he told Ken Tynan, 'is as big a lie as the deliberate fantasies I construct. It's based on the fallacy of naturalism. There's a direct line of descent which leads you straight down to the dregs of bad theatre, bad thinking and bad feeling.'[29] It is an important remark, shedding light on both his earlier work and the more recent *Night and Day* and *The Real Thing*, as we shall see later. His description of his plays as 'deliberate fantasies' is as illuminating as his strictures against naturalism, and the phrase can, perhaps, best be glossed by an examination of two articles in *Scene* on the novelist and playwright Muriel Spark. In these two pieces Stoppard's rejection of naturalism is married with an equally Formalist notion of how its pretensions can best be exposed.

In the first, Stoppard (using the pseudonym William Boot, the innocent abroad in Africa who, in Evelyn Waugh's *Scoop*, stimulates an examination of journalism in the way that Jacob Milne does in *Night and Day*) interviews Spark during rehearsals of her *Doctors of Philosophy*. Spark is described as a writer whose imagination accommodates 'humans with one foot out of this world and accepts unblinkingly situations that trespass on the supernatural'.[30] Later in the same issue Stoppard reviews the play. To Spark, he explains, reality is a figment of the imagination: 'The idea is that we are so conditioned to life's accepted norm that we reject a multitude of aberrations which, did we not blink at those precise moments, would reveal human absurdity and, perhaps, a supernatural power.'[31] In *Rosencrantz and Guildenstern are Dead* the more incisive of the two deracinated courtiers uses the image of the eye. 'All your life you live so close to truth,' says Guildenstern, 'it becomes a permanent blur in the corner of your eye, and when something nudges it into outline it is like being ambushed by a grotesque.'[32] What attracts Stoppard to Spark is the fact that her world is structured by opposition: that opposition between habitual, mechanised perception and its breakdown which is experienced directly by Guildenstern and which is identified as the province of literariness by the Russian Formalists. Stoppard's review of *Doctors of Philosophy* is a document of great interest, helping to define and explain those moments of ambush in his own drama when habit is broken down.

Stoppard points out that to treat reality in the way Spark does is not an original thought. She does, however, have 'more fun with it than most, mainly because she does not treat it as a thesis, but as a premise. She does not attempt to prove it or to promulgate it; she simply accepts it. And toys with it.'[33] Stoppard's own thought is not original. The notion that the artist should not attempt to promulgate a thesis is anticipated by Chekhov, who remarks in a letter that it is possible to confuse the solution of a question and the correct setting of a question: 'the latter alone is obligatory for the artist'.[34] Beckett voices the same idea in championing the poet Denis Devlin against the 'great crossword public' and its 'morbid dread of sphinxes' clamouring for 'solution clapped on problem like a snuffer on a candle'.[35] However, the formulation is probably most accessible in another writer with a directly traceable influence on Stoppard. 'No artist' announces Wilde in the preface to *The Picture of Dorian Gray*, 'desires to prove anything. Even things that are true can be proved.'[36] What is in-teresting, however, is Stoppard's emphasis on 'fun'; that cancellation of habit which Spark displays is, for him, a comic undertaking.

'This belief (I assume it is a belief, but it would not matter very much if it were a literary device) makes her novels distinctive and disturbing, a world of everyday reality made brittle by the admission of the unreal.' The parenthesis is important: Stoppard is concerned not with the religious overtones of Spark's 'vision' but with her literary practices and the implications of her playwrighting appren-ticeship. Confined to novel-writing, Spark solves the formal problems involved in casting a strange light on the quotidian world. On stage she fails. The play groans with her efforts to catch her audience unawares, to nudge the pale blur into outline. The plot, Stoppard complains, gets curiouser and curiouser, 'never more so or more suddenly than in the nearly fatal second act where Mrs Spark chooses to make two characters step outside the action of the play and, as a crude example of unreality, expose the scenery as plain scenery.'[37] Some weeks later, in reviewing Edna O'Brien's *A Cheap Bunch of Nice Flowers*, Stoppard took the opportunity to return to his points about Spark. Like *Doctors of Philosophy*, O'Brien's is 'the first stage-play of a young novelist, and it can hardly be a coincidence that the two share the same virtues and faults: the final effect is of a worth-while literary achievement which barely survives its own assault on the technical canons of stagecraft.' He adds that after the first night of *Doctors of Philosophy* 'these tricks were done away with and the play worked better as a straightforward and literate comedy.'[38]

We are here at the crux of Stoppard's thinking on the relationship between the writer and the forms of expression available to him. His Formalist theatre is firmly based on an awareness of the need to re-employ established modes of procedure, to marry critical questioning with a well-versed conservatism. The lesson suggested by Beckett's *Happy Days* is repeated. Spark and Wheeler occupy the two poles between which the artist, to operate successfully, must function. Spark's dismissal of stage convention takes place in a vacuum: her deviation from the traditional canon does not perform a critical function because that canon is not itself sufficiently evoked. Spark's audience is not offered the requisite awareness of Jakobson's two orders, and Stoppard's remarks in *Scene* are an implicit and uncon-scious reiteration of Jakobson's insistence that it is only against the background of tradition that innovation is conceived and, by extension, perceived. Like the Formalists Stoppard suggests that each work of literature (and not just Literature as a whole) is a system defined by relation: just as the work which breaks rules is of interest only if other writing continues to observe them, so those moments of innovation within the individual work are of value only in relation to those parts of the work which lead us to expect no such departure. For Spark's play to have made 'brittle' the world of the stage by the admission of the unexpected, Stoppard required from it a far more pronounced sense of the facility of the familiar. Hugh Wheeler, on the other hand, represents a victory of the tidy mind over the questioning spirit: *Big Fish, Little Fish* fails to play off innovation against the traditional canon and its form remains, as a consequence, serene, uninteresting, unobserved.

Spark and O'Brien, Stoppard implies, are unable to evoke the two orders because of their inexperience: as apprentice playwrights they are unable, in the first place, to meet the demands of the traditional canon. Innovation should be the signature of the artist's will, a deliberate choice, a bid for freedom. However, in failing to muster the discipline of their craft, Spark and O'Brien confuse freedom with delinquency. Stoppard himself, is, of course, proud of the diligence with which *he* has mustered the discipline, congratulating himself on his craftsmanship as well as his 'originality'. 'There's a kind of play that I don't write and Rattigan doesn't either,' he says, announcing a seemingly unlikely admiration, 'a play where one says all these outmoded forms of drama are such a bore and I'm going to free the whole thing from these fetters . . . and the result is an absolute boring mess.'[39] The same point is made, more obliquely, by his description of his plays as 'deliberate fantasies': the phrase signals not simply a departure from naturalism, but a departure that is 'deliberate' in the double sense of being both willed and considered or disciplined.

Stoppard's radio-play *Artist Descending a Staircase* addresses itself explicitly to the problem of artistic innovation and freedom and, in so doing, makes use of the polar extremes of delinquency and conformity personified in the pages of *Scene* by Muriel Spark and Hugh Wheeler.

Beauchamp, one of three artists who carry the central debate, busies himself with tonal art, taped recordings of apparently unrelated and frequently unidentifiable sounds. To Beauchamp the mind is a *tabula rasa* upon which has been inscribed the manifesto of realism; man is capable of new experience if his means of expression is liberated. 'Art,' he declaims, tramping through France at the outbreak of the Great War, 'consists of constant surprise. Art should never conform. Art should break its promises. Art is nothing to do with expertise: doing something well is no excuse for doing the expected.'[40] Sixty years on he tells Donner that if his tape were played on the radio it would seem a meaningless noise 'because it fulfils no expectations: people have been taught to expect certain kinds of insight but not others. The first duty of the artist is to capture the radio station,' (p. 20). He points out that Donner, who claims his art is for Everyman, selects his public as carefully as he does, 'but my tapes have greater mystery – they elude dogs, parrots, clerks and the greater part of mankind,' (p. 20). The modish iconoclasm of his youth has hardened into the obstinate, priggish delinquency of his dotage.

'I very much enjoyed my years in that child's garden of easy victories known as the avant garde,' sniffs Donner, 'but I am now engaged in the infinitely more difficult task of painting what the eye sees,' (p. 19). Beauchamp has not taught new insight but has simply left his audience far behind. Donner's return to realism after the heady Dadaism of his youth and his anguished experimentation with ceramic food and edible art, is dictated by his need to forge a link between the activities of the artist and the lives led by his fellow men. 'I have returned to traditional values,' he tells Beauchamp, 'that is where the true history of art continues to lie, not in your small jokes,' (p. 22). Donner celebrates, then, those forms we have canonised as the real. By conforming to the expectations of Everyman, he believes he has rediscovered both the link between art and life and the criterion which decides the value of the work of art.

To Martello, Donner's broodings and answers are as absurd as Beauchamp's. His position, in essence, is a criticism of the polar extremes represented by his two friends. 'Painting,' insists Martello, 'is a technique and can be learned, like playing the piano. But how,' he asks, and the importance of this question to Stoppard cannot be easily overestimated, 'can you teach someone to think in a certain way? – to paint an utterly simple shape in order to ambush the mind with something unexpected about that shape by hanging it in a frame and forcing you to see it, as it were, for the first time,' (p. 39). Again Stoppard uses the image of the ambush to describe that moment in which, according to Guildenstern, the pale blur in the corner of the eye is nudged into outline. To the idea of ambush the notion of 'framing' is, of course, of paramount importance: only when an audience's expectations are aroused in certain directions (when experience is 'framed' for them) can they be surprised from another. Significantly, Stoppard describes his own plays as advancing through 'a series of small, large and microscopic ambushes.'[41]

Martello, of course, is suggesting an opposition which is at the root of Formalist thinking: that opposition drawn by Shklovsky between 'seeing' and 'recognising' an object. What distinguishes Martello and the Formalists from Beauchamp is the contention that we only 'see' by virtue of a sudden awareness of the failings of our previous acts of 'recognition'. Beauchamp's tonal art encourages no such provisional recognition. It is the relation established between recognition and seeing which enables the work to perform a critical function; the delinquency of Beauchamp, on the other hand, must remain purely gestural.

It is no mere coincidence that Martello is the most consistently humorous of Stoppard's unholy trinity. His humour, characteristically, is ambush: the strategic use of the unexpected word or phrase. Martello has a way with clichés: his best jokes manoeuvre them deftly into position before nudging them into outline. 'My brain is on a flying trapeze that outstrips all possibilities of action,' he claims, apparently denigrating his own achievements as an artist, 'Mental acrobatics, Beauchamp – I have achieved nothing but mental acrobatics – *nothing!* – whereas you, however wrongly and for whatever reason, came to grips with life at least this once, and killed Donner,' (p. 16). Martello's joke makes us take a second look at language, language that is made strange by his laughter. He uses cliché to hang language in a frame, forcing us to see it, as it were, for the first time.

This is, perhaps, best seen in an important exchange with Donner, when Martello shows him his sculptured figure. Martello's figure is a concrete metaphor, or series of concrete metaphors: she sports hair of ripe corn, teeth of pearls, feathers upon her swan-like neck. When Donner realises that it is meant to represent Sophie, the blind girl with whom he had fallen in love but who had attached herself to Beauchamp, he cannot contain his anger at her 'beauty mocked in death' by Martello's 'contemptible artistic presumptions':

DONNER (*by now nearly weeping*):   Oh, Sophie . . . I cannot
    think of beauty without remembering your innocent grace,
    your hair like . . .
MARTELLO: Ripe corn –
DONNER: Gold. Your tragic gaze – eyes like –
MARTELLO: Stars –

DONNER: Bottomless pools, and when you laughed –
MARTELLO: Teeth like pearls –
DONNER: It was like a silver bell whose sound parted your pale
           ruby lips –
MARTELLO: *A silver bell!* – yes! – behind her breasts –
DONNER: – were like –
MARTELLO: – ripe pears –
DONNER: Firm young apples.
MARTELLO: Pears – For heaven's sake control yourself, Donner,
           those are real artificial pearls –
           (*Pearls bouncing* – DONNER *thumping, gasping . . .*)

                                                        (pp. 28–9)

Martello has made language strange by giving the metaphor concrete
form. In a sense, his act of defamiliarisation has been achieved by
the technique of *obnaženie priëma*, the device laid bare by its
repetition in a new, incongruous, physical context. The cliché is
nudged into grotesque outline. The central irony of the scene, of
course, comes from the juxtaposition of Donner's heartfelt outpour-
ings and Martello's ironic observations. At a pitch of emotion,
Donner expresses himself 'naturally' in clichés not entirely dissimilar
to those parodied by Martello. This is another of those 'looking-
glass adventures' which Irving Wardle finds so disconcerting. By
cancelling Martello's clichés with Donner's, Stoppard completes the
equation of artifice. Donner, who will soon turn from edible art (a
sugar Venus de Milo) to painting what the eye sees, falls foul of an
ironic reversal as he unwittingly demonstrates that the 'real' may
only be the familiar we recognise at hand – in this case the stale
familiarity of the literary cliché.
  Martello admits that the only thing to be said in defence of his
figure is that you 'can smile at it' (p. 27). Martello has grasped the
intimate connection between criticism and laughter which characterises Stoppard's own Formalist endeavours, and which the latter finds
similarly distinctive in Beckett's work. To a certain extent, Martello
travesties Stoppard's own procedures, addressing himself to the same
problem, asking himself the same questions. His is a critical reaction
to the stark alternatives represented by Beauchamp and Donner: his
notion of 'frame' counters the delinquency of the former, and that
of ambush the conformism of the latter. In parody Martello, like
Stoppard, marries the comic and the critical aspects of his
imagination.

Stoppard's articles in *Scene* sketch out an aesthetics of engagement. His basic premise is clear: artistic freedom cannot exist in a
vacuum, it is a function of the artist's engagement with the forms at
his disposal, an engagement which facilitates a concomitant critical
response on the part of his audience. Before we turn to an examination of the ways in which this critical premise informs the parodic
strategies of Stoppard's own drama and his only novel to date, one
more article from the pages of *Scene* deserves detailed attention. It
charts Stoppard's encounter with what he has described to me as
'the first play I'd ever seen which I would have liked to have written
and thought that I might have written'.[42] That play is James Saunders'
Next Time I'll Sing To You.

II

Art, James Saunders has said, is that region of experience where
strange questions can be asked and strange answers given. Theatre
is a 'playspace where you can ask silly or serious questions about
life, death, time, space, freedom and compulsion, what it is to see
and hear, what words really are'. It is, he continues, unconsciously
echoing the Russian Formalists, 'a rebellion against life as a mechanical operation'.[43] *Next Time I'll Sing To You* is Saunders' finest
play, in which theatre as playspace is most effectively used to ask
facetiously serious questions about what words really are and fiction
really is. The play shot Saunders to brief celebrity in the cold winter
of 1963; overnight he became one of the most lauded of the young
playwrights following in the footsteps of Beckett and Osborne, the
twin catalysts of that explosion of excitement which lit up the London
stage at the end of one decade and the beginning of the next. Indeed,
such was the impression that *Next Time I'll Sing To You* made upon
Tom Stoppard at a formative stage of his career that its influence on
Rosencrantz and Guildenstern are Dead, the play which first brought
Stoppard the celebrity which had once been Saunders', is unmistakable. Inspection of the two plays, in the light of Stoppard's remarks
in *Scene*, will expose the error in Tim Brassell's claim that, despite
certain surface similarities, 'there seems no basis for an extensive
comparison' between them.[44]

The enthusiasm of the first audience of *Next Time I'll Sing To You*
is reflected in the notices which greeted its opening at the New Arts
in 1963. For Peter Lewis, in the *Daily Mail*, it was a 'feat of brilli-

ance', and Ken Tynan was almost as complimentary in *The Observer* where he described it, in homage to Pirandello, as 'Actors in Search of a Character'. Harold Hobson hailed it in *The Sunday Times* as a turning point in contemporary drama, as the miraculous resuscitation of a moribund London stage dominated by slavish imitations of Beckett: Saunders kicks the coffin aside 'and the supposed corpse stands before you, sober and his face a'shining, full of life and vigour and hope'.[45]

There were, inevitably, a few voices raised in dissent. It was one of those 'riddle-me-ree pieces' according to W. A. Darlington, who sidled off stage with a mumbled 'let's just say it was not my kind of play'. Philip Hope-Wallace, on the other hand, could not resist taking a swipe at those who enjoyed it rather more than he did. In the dark of the auditorium Hope-Wallace abandoned himself to the 'pirandellian frisson' of *Next Time I'll Sing To You*, 'such as it is and it still didn't silence the gigglers who are the bane of this special club theatre'. Ultimately, the play, for Hope-Wallace, was too much of a tease: 'We are not told enough. The fatuities jar instead of bringing out the deeper echoes and at the end there are few reverberations left.'[46]

The tone of such criticism – dismissing the play as wilfully impenetrable and condemning it for withholding conclusions the audience has a right to expect – is indicative of an attitude to drama and the potentialities of theatre which is denied by *Next Time I'll Sing To You*. The play assembles a group of actors to present the strange life of Jimmy Mason, the hermit of Great Canfield who immured himself in a ramshackle hut for thirty-six years. One of their number, Dust, turns his scorn upon the audience, claiming that they are salivating for answers, killing time till the 'great mushroom cloud of enlightenment that'll lighten up for a moment their pallid cheeks,' and will send them home to their bedtime cocoa 'full of hope for Man's tomorrow'.[47] Ken Tynan shrank from what he called these 'glibly disparaging remarks', but in so doing he made the point which had eluded, among others, Darlington and Hope-Wallace: Saunders' view of Man's estate, Tynan insists, is that he is solitary 'but sacred, and no fiction can encompass him'.[48] Included among those fictions which can but fail to encompass the mystery of Jimmy Mason ('a mind locked in twelve hundred grammes of brain locked in a quarter of an inch of skull,' (p. 35)) – is *Next Time I'll Sing To You* itself. Paramount among the strange questions it asks is a question about its own status as a guide to the truth. Saunders' play is a willing investigation of the constraints we embrace to make our lives livable. It takes measure of the compass of our fictions.

Among the gigglers in the New Arts on Opening Night, reviewing the play for *Scene*, and irritating the man from the *Guardian*, was Tom Stoppard. His review is a fascinating document, shedding light on his own work as well as that of Saunders: it shows him responding with alacrity to the very nature of Saunders' theatre. He describes the author as a man not concerned with reality, who 'leaves no stone unturned, expecting to find the truth not beneath any one of them but in what the stones look like the wrong way up'.[49] Turning the stone upside down is exactly what Stoppard attempts in *Rosencrantz and Guildenstern are Dead* as he exposes the hidden underside of the pre-text, *Hamlet*.

Saunders' achievement, according to Stoppard, lies in equating 'the basic eccentricity of his play with the particular problem it tackles'. Here form itself is the problem: it has been subsumed under content. At the heart of the work is a *critical* undertaking: a dismantling of the pretensions of literary discourse. 'The truth of the hermit,' writes Stoppard, 'is not to be approached from the outside in. That is the point, and ultimately,' he continues, in familiar vein, 'all the dazzling divisions, cross-indexed and self-cancelling, are beside it.'[50] In Saunders Stoppard has recognised a kindred spirit, an artist of literary hypersensitivity, asking what words really are and drama really is. The debate in Saunders' play about the pretensions and the duplicity of art – and its focus on the problem of identity – will reappear in *Rosencrantz and Guildenstern are Dead*. Stoppard takes it up and works upon it – and does so in terms of a shared analogy and shared imagery. Indeed, Stoppard will borrow directly from the play recently dismissed by Irving Wardle as a clutter of 'absurdist *bric-à-brac*'.[51]

Stoppard's Guildenstern is repeatedly ambushed by his terrified sense of the sheer inevitability of what is happening around him. He advises Rosencrantz to relax and let the logic of the action unfold: 'If we start being arbitrary it'll just be a shambles: at least, let us hope so. Because if we happened, just happened to discover, or even suspect, that our spontaneity was part of their order, we'd know that we were lost' (pp. 42–3). Deprived of the power to disrupt events, the two attendant lords would disappear as completely as cause detached from effect. In *Scene* Stoppard described Saunders' Dust as suffering from the repressed fury of schizophrenia, 'the knowledge that his spontaneity is part of a nightly repeated plan'.[52]

Indeed, in discussing the problem of identity in terms of the control over events which the individual can hope to achieve, Stoppard's debt to Saunders is obvious.

As an actor engaged by Rudge, the 'fragmentary Hamlet' who has engineered this 'lopsided once-nightly little dreamworld' (p. 17) in the hope of exploring the life of Jimmy Mason, Dust is aware that a point is reached where control is relinquished and the self can no longer separate itself from the role. He compares himself to a steel ball rolling down a hill and, when warmed up, will cry 'It's running, it's running. The ball's beginning to roll,' (p. 11) and will compare himself to an aeroplane, ecstatic at the moment of take-off: 'I shall be flying free, I shall imagine I am in control,' (p. 11). Yet Dust knows that this sense of control is illusory, and that it is dependent on the arrival on stage of Rudge, the man who has written his lines and his ecstasy for him. Sourly, Dust ackowledges the script as his destiny, assuring Lizzie that he has no designs upon her body, 'Not that if I were *written* rapacious I shouldn't have a shot at it' (p. 9). When Rudge enters he makes it clear that he has no more control over the proceedings than the actors he has assembled to re-enact their failure to begin a play about the hermit of Great Canfield: 'you think because I'm given control, I'm in control. You're old enough to know better. Very well, stick to your fiction. I'm in control. I'm God' (p. 18). He challenges Dust to try being in control: 'Try going through the motions of doing what you want instead of what you have to, knowing it'll come to the same' (p. 18).

Stoppard's Player willingly relinquishes control, with none of the repressed fury of Saunders' players. 'We have no control,' he says proudly, 'Tonight we play to the court. Or the night after. Or to the tavern. Or not' (p. 18). 'Don't you see,' he asks, 'We're *actors* – we're the opposite of people' (p. 45). Rosencrantz and Guildenstern, however, fight to preserve the distinction between actor and agent, to preserve the short-lived sense of purpose which will give their actions meaning. 'This is all getting rather undisciplined,' murmurs Guildenstern as he looks for the letter to the English King, 'We must not lose control' (p. 77). Control, unfortunately, when claimed, brings the pair face to face with their own uncertainty. 'All right, we know you're in there!' screams Rosencrantz in an attempted seizure of initiative. 'Come out talking!' Nothing happens: 'We have no control. None at all' (p. 51).

Stoppard also duplicates Saunders' use of momentum as an analogy to describe the circumscription of initiative. The performance of *Hamlet* in which the pair have been entangled rolls forward with distressing impetus. 'Very impressive,' says Guildenstern sarcastically to his partner, 'Yes, I thought your direct informal approach was going to stop this thing dead in its tracks there' (p. 54). Aboard the ship for England, Guildenstern tells Rosencrantz to request a tune from the recorder-player inside the barrel: 'Quick, before we lose our momentum' (p. 82). As the play moves towards its fatal climax, Guildenstern comes to see this sense of control as illusory. 'We've travelled too far,' he mutters, 'and our momentum has taken over; we move idly towards eternity, without possibility of reprieve or hope of explanation' (pp. 87–8).

It is, however, Stoppard's most direct borrowing from Saunders which best captures the dilemma in which his central characters find themselves. 'I wish someone would tell me what to do,' (p. 12) whines Saunders' Lizzie. She recalls asking her sister for instructions: 'She didn't understand it either. Don't worry about nothing, she said, just act natural' (p. 12). Her cry is taken up by Guildenstern: 'we don't know what's going on, or what to do with ourselves. We don't know how to *act*.' 'Act natural,' (p. 48) counsels the Player, wilfully confusing action with acting, and the agent with the actor. The pun leaves the central question unanswered: is there any possibility of a spontaneous act, or is the agent's sense of purpose just capitulation to a logic unstoppable and *absurd?*

Guildenstern is appalled by the notion of *order* without *meaning* and it is these two terms which shape the debate in *Next Time I'll Sing To You* about the nature of art. On one side is the view of art as essentially revelatory, which sees the aesthetic object as an ordered microcosm reflecting the pattern of the macrocosm; in opposition is the claim that the categories of art are entirely fictional and a specious denial of disorder. Rudge's dream is a dream of order, an order made explicit by the ministrations of art. 'To impose order on nature, this was to be my life's work,' (p. 55) he recalls of his youthful hopes of a career as a landscape gardener. 'Simplicity is all I ask for,' he insists, 'the question answered, the doubt put to rest, the fact explained – logical simplicity' (p. 56). But Rudge knows that logical simplicity is not solution but travesty; he makes the point by providing Dust with a neat reversal of the analogy of art as mirror. If you hold a mirror to the face of life, claims Dust, it preens itself and strikes the noble attitude, 'But out of sight, with the other hand, it quietly scratches its bottom. Suppose now a full-length mirror; which is real, the nobility in the face or the hand, scratching?' (p.

66). Art creates the reality it claims to reflect; its meanings are arbitrary.

In Stoppard's play the problems resurface in Guildenstern's encounter with *Hamlet*. His responses to the action which sweeps in from the wings argue his search for a significance in events to justify the pattern of art, proclaiming *order* as *meaning*. In the Player, of course, he meets a suitable opponent. Truth, claims the Player, is just the currency of living: 'There may be nothing behind it, but it doesn't make any difference so long as it is honoured' (p. 48). Guildenstern yearns for *meaning*, while the Player will settle for *order*, calmly relinquishing control if that is what is required. The conflict between the two is mirrored in their debate about art, as Stoppard pursues Saunders' determination to ask what words really are and what drama really is.

'There's a design at work in all art – surely you know that?' the Player says to Guildenstern, 'Events must play themselves out to aesthetic, moral and logical conclusion' (p. 57). Art is remorseless in its demands: 'we aim,' he continues, icily, 'at the point where everyone who is marked for death dies' (p. 57). The art of the Player's life is the murderous relish with which he obeys the dictates of this sensationally familiar world. Guildenstern's quarrel with him is about the nature of the design which is in art. In mirroring life it must reveal meaning and significance, not just impose its own shape. When the players enact a theatrical slaughter Guildenstern can discern no truth in their cheap melodrama; 'it doesn't catch them unawares,' he says of a potential audience, 'and start the whisper in their skulls that says – "One day you are going to die" ' (p. 61). He plunges a toy dagger into the Player and, along with Stoppard's audience, is fooled by the mechanics of cheap melodrama. After a brief silence the tragedians applaud as the Player stands and brushes himself down. In upholding the rights of life against the deformations of cheap art, in attempting to get the actor to come to grips with life at least once, by killing him, Guildenstern unwittingly demonstrates the fictional nature of what he conceives to be the real.

In asking what drama really is, in following the metadramatic strategies of *Next Time I'll Sing To You*, *Rosencrantz and Guildenstern are Dead* conducts a similar investigation into the notion of theatre as a metaphor for life. This preoccupation links the related concerns with the problem of identity and the nature of art. By turning *Hamlet* upside down Stoppard asks whether tragedy is an adequate metaphor for the way we live our lives. It is Guildenstern

who says, as we have already seen, 'All your life you live so close
to truth, it becomes a permanent blur in the corner of your eye, and
when something nudges it into outline it is like being ambushed by
a grotesque' (p. 28). Stoppard 'defamiliarises' *Hamlet;* he performs
a critical function which nudges it into new and unfamiliar outline.

On a more complex level, Stoppard explores the theatre-life metaphor by examining the related roles of critic and artist. Guildenstern's
personality is defined by his relationship to *Hamlet*, by his fluctuation
(and here we can see a parallel with Stoppard's description of the
plight of the Beckettian refugee) between his earnest desire to make
sense of, to criticise, the action around him, and his occasional
capitulation to a design he accepts but does not understand. 'To be
taken in hand and led,' he says, sacrificing the struggle for freedom
for the comforts of compulsion, 'like being a child again. . . . It's
like being given a prize, an extra slice of childhood when you least
expect it' (p. 29). 'One of the reasons that the play turned out to
work so well, I think,' said Stoppard in a television interview, 'is
that the predicament of the characters coincides with the predicament
of the playwright.'[53] In fact, in *Rosencrantz and Guildenstern are
Dead*, Stoppard handles his predicament rather more successfully
than his two main characters: by turning the stone upside down, to
see what it looks like the wrong way up, Stoppard demonstrates that
initiative which Guildenstern denies. By criticising *Hamlet*, in effect,
Stoppard disrupts the internal power-structure of the work, elevating
to a position of unwonted dominance the play's own continual questioning of the nature of art, its own thoroughgoing awareness of the
degree to which life and action are conditioned by the forms we
have adopted to make it comprehensible. Stoppard succeeds where
Guildenstern fails: he does not act *in* Shakespeare's drama, he acts
upon it.

Rosencrantz and Guildenstern are Dead asserts itself within the
overall design of *Hamlet;* it probes the possibility of freedom while
acknowledging the fact of constraint. The particular instance reflects
the general case: in Stoppard's plays fictions are not so much the
subject as the *condition* of the creative act. It is his stylish observation
of the demands of specific genres which marks so clearly his depar-
tures from them, within the same play. In *Rosencrantz and Guildenstern are Dead* the presence of a specific text, *Hamlet*, invokes that
heavy weight of our fictions as interpretive constructs which is, as
Stoppard declares in *Scene*, the necessary precondition for our liberation from them. In *Next Time I'll Sing To You* James Saunders asks

serious and silly questions about freedom and compulsion and in so doing asks what words really are and drama really is. The importance of the play to *Rosencrantz and Guildenstern are Dead* can be gauged not only by the extent of direct borrowing, but also by the rigour with which Stoppard relates the problem of freedom – explicitly in the problem of personal identity, implicitly in the example of his own creative act – to his own metadramatic preoccupations.

In 1964 Stoppard was awarded a Ford Foundation grant and was installed in a mansion in West Berlin where he worked on turning 'a sort of Shakespearean pastiche'[54] into a one-act play. Three other writers worked alongside Stoppard: Derek Marlowe, Piers Paul Reid and James Saunders. Stoppard showed 'Rosencrantz and Guildenstern meet King Lear' to Saunders and was encouraged by the older man to turn it into a full-length play. Back in England, Stoppard had an extract from the new play performed by the Questors at Ealing, the company which produced all of Saunders' plays and encouraged him to experiment with *Next Time I'll Sing to You*. Given Stoppard's habit of revising through rehearsal and performance it is possible that the text continued to grow under Saunders' influence and, perhaps, because of his presence and that of actors familiar with his work. 'There is a secret in Art, isn't there?' Stoppard has said, 'and the secret consists of what the artist has secretly and privately done. You will tumble some and not others.'[55]

Fifteen years after *Next Time I'll Sing To You* was hailed as a milestone in contemporary drama Saunders noted that 'they think a lot of my work in Germany: that's how I live, really – German royalties and adapting other people's work for television'. He comforted himself with the thought that there were only a few years before he got his pension and claimed that he had carried on writing 'because there is no alternative – playwriting is quite literally the only thing I can do'.[56] Ken Tynan notes that a rift has developed between Stoppard and Saunders since the mid-sixties. When Stoppard first became famous, recalls Saunders, 'he gave a series of expensive lunches at the Café Royal to keep in touch with his old pals. I thought that was pretty ostentatious behaviour. Meeting him nowadays I do feel a sort of cut-off.' At this point, Tynan says, he made a gesture like a portcullis descending. 'I don't think he's overrated,' Saunders went on, 'as much as that many other writers are underrated. He has distracted attention from people who have an equal right to it.'[57] Perhaps Saunders had seen what the artist had secretly and privately done.

3
The Novel as Hinged Mirror

Stoppard told Giles Gordon in 1968 that, of the countless books he had read and plays he had sat through, there were very, very few which offered an experience differing from all the other experiences to be expected from books and plays: 'There are very few books which seem to me to get away from what everybody else is doing. I think that a book like *At Swim-Two-Birds* is going to influence writers for a century. . . . How far back can one go?' he wondered, '*Tristram Shandy, Ulysses, At Swim-Two-Birds?*'[1] Stoppard's yardstick for measuring the value of a novel is, then, the same as he had used in *Scene* for assessing a play: the remark restates his preoccupation with the need to shake the reader or spectator out of his deep, detached sense of familiarity with what is set before him. The work he admires is that which, by an act of criticism, distances itself from its background; his praise of *Tristram Shandy* emphasises his closeness to the Formalists in this respect: Shklovsky was fascinated with the way that Sterne freed himself from the conventions of the novel by parodying them.[2] Stoppard's list of books which 'get away from what everybody else is doing' (and which, paradoxically, themselves become models for duplication) is also an implicit acknowledgement of the debt he owes to Flann O'Brien, whose *At Swim-Two-Birds* has a direct influence upon Stoppard's only novel to date, *Lord Malquist and Mr Moon* (1966).

O'Brien described his novel as 'a belly-laugh or a sort of high-class literary pretentious slush, depending on how you look at it.'[3] *At Swim-Two-Birds* is indeed a belly-laugh at literature, a mocking disavowal of our established 'transcriptions of reality'. 'Think,' says Myles NaGopoleen, or rather Flann O'Brien, or rather Brian O'Nolan, 'of the illiterate's acute observation of the real world as distinct from the pale, print-interpreted thing that means life for most of us.'[4] In *At Swim-Two-Birds* O'Brien is concerned with emphasising for the reader the implications of print-interpreted

40

reality and of print-conditioned perception. The novel is a work of self-delighting formal complexity, a kaleidoscopic array of styles arranged into stories within stories sealed in the envelope of the *nearest* narrator's biographical reminiscences. In the semi-humorous aesthetic theories of his student narrator O'Brien supplies both a defence of the anti-novel as artistic form and a parody of his own procedure. The belly-laugh is on O'Brien as well.

O'Brien's narrator rails at the despotism and the deception of the realist novel which imposes a particular perspective on the reader and induces him or her 'to be outwitted in a shabby fashion and caused to experience a real concern for the fortunes of illusory characters'.[5] What the narrator calls for is a text which gives the reader his freedom by acknowledging its own arbitrary nature; it should be, then, 'a self-evident sham to which the reader could regulate at will the degree of credulity' (p. 25). This anticipates Roland Barthes, whose 'writerly' text is a self-evident sham which seeks to exercise no despotism over the reader but which gives him an active role to play in the production of meaning. The narrator also outlines his own facetious notion of intertextuality; convinced that most writers spend their time saying what has already been said (and usually said much better), he declares that the modern novel should be regarded as a work of reference and the entire corpus of existing literature as 'a limbo from which discerning authors could draw their characters as required, creating only when they failed to find a suitable existing puppet' (p. 25). This, of course, is something of a blueprint for Stoppard's own procedure in *Rosencrantz and Guildenstern are Dead* and *Travesties;* it is also a recognition that literature itself is the problem which the critical text must address. The narrator lays down a self-consciousness of approach which, by displaying the propensity of literature to duplicate itself, will turn a vice into a virtue.

An extra dimension to the narrator's justification of his novel is provided by his claim that 'the novel was inferior to the play inasmuch as it lacked the outward accidents of illusion' (p. 25). Once again his mocking pronouncements anticipate the findings of 'legitimate' criticism: 'The theatre,' says Christopher Bigsby in his book on Joe Orton, 'constitutes a naturally reflexive setting, one that might seem more ideally suited to the exploration of many postmodern concerns than is the novel. The fictive quality of drama is, after all, inescapable; as with crustacea, its skeleton is always on the outside.'[6] O'Brien's narrator strives to incorporate into his text the critical presence of illusion-breakers, to turn the novel's skeleton from the inside out.

At Swim-Two-Birds, the novel as self-evident sham, is a patchwork of styles, none of which is allowed to entrap the reader. Interpolations from *A Conspectus of the Arts and Sciences* and *The Athenian Oracle* vie for attention with multifarious parody – of Westerns, travel brochures, journalese, translations of Gaelic legends, mediaeval homilies and the 'realistic dialogue' of the Dublin pub. A proposed style is established only to be knocked down, its 'naturalness' denied. Everything is cancelled out as the novel is assembled, according to a principle of composition Stoppard's admiration for which we have already seen. At all times the narrator is determined to break down his prose into its component parts. Often the text simply comments in general terms upon the effect it is creating and the means it has chosen; on occasions it is more detailed (proudly pointing out, for example, instances of synecdoche and anaphora). O'Brien consistently foregrounds the stylistic device for comic effect, and this critical dismantling of the pretensions of style is extended to the plot. The novel repeatedly interrupts the flow of its events, introducing general synopses of things too difficult to describe, admitting the loss of certain pages, inserting summaries of both what has gone and what is to come.

According to one critic, the narrative and stylistic gymnastics of *At Swim-Two-Birds* make explicit 'the narrator's refusal to adhere to the fiction that only one way of seeing may be selected and sustained'.[7] This openness of mind, an inability or refusal to canvass experience, produces the terror of the inverted world in O'Brien's *The Third Policeman* as well as the comic freedom of *At Swim-Two-Birds*. As a humorist, O'Brien is at pains to suggest that reality is a far more complex business than our pale, print-interpreted apprehension of it allows. In *Lord Malquist and Mr Moon* Stoppard's aristocratic and latter-day dandy claims that we live so close to absurdity that it escapes our notice: ' "But if the sky were turned into a great mirror and we caught ourselves in it unawares, we should not be able to look each other in the face." He closed his eyes. "Since we cannot hope for order let us withdraw with style from the chaos." '[8] Malquist's is one, calculated reaction to the *defamiliarisation* of those structures which have maintained our comfortable notion of the real. In Mr Moon, his incompetent amanuensis and hired Boswell, Stoppard depicts another, and more painfully comic. Significantly, the novel (which was published in the same week, according to

Stoppard, as *Rosencrantz and Guildenstern are Dead* opened in Edinburgh[9]) contains a central debate over the nature and pretensions of literary art, that mirror in which we may recognise ourselves or, suddenly, *see* the hand scratching. The novel emerges from a critical engagement with realism in the same way as the comic strategies of *At Swim-Two-Birds*.

O'Brien's narrator gives us three openings to his novel. O'Brien himself gives us four, including an introduction to the narrator, retired into the privacy of his mind and pondering his art behind vacant-looking eyes. Stoppard, in turn, outdoes both and allows his novel five separate openings. In the first we are presented with Malquist and Moon in the former's carriage, clearing a path through the encroaching city. Stoppard's prose is inseminated with Malquist's fastidious, fin-de-siècle aestheticism: 'He took a grip (lilac-gloved) on the door-frame (rosewood, mother-of-pearl) as the pair of pigeon-coloured horses rocked the coach up Whitehall under the mourning-flags and across the Square, kicking dun-coloured pigeons into the air' (p. 8). This is prose as self-evident sham: the pigeon-coloured horses and dun-coloured pigeons strike a deliberate balance in which each description cancels the other out. This principle of composition continues to dominate as Malquist's *bon mots* are cancelled out by Moon's incompetence. ' "My pearl pinned to my lapel," ' states Malquist, ' "is of a colour described by my jeweller in literal translation from his native Chinese as sun-kissed dewdrop on earlobe of bathing-in-pool maiden" ' (p. 10). In Moon's hands this succulent verbalisation is reduced to grotesque travesty: 'His hand wrote on as far as *pink as pearl in ear of Chinese bathing beauty*, at which point its memory gave out' (p. 11). The first opening contains, in little, the movement which characterises the first section of the novel: a proposed style is established and, almost instantaneously, is refuted.

The halting, parenthetical self-consciousness of the initial opening is replaced by a parody of Westerns as we meet Long John Slaughter and Jasper Jones, lineal descendants of O'Brien's urban cowboys, Slug Willard and Shorty Andrews. This, in turn, gives way to a style of menacing factuality describing what at first seems to be the agonies of a thirst-racked desert-traveller (in fact, an alcoholic stumbling through a London park). Next, the tribulations of the Risen Christ are conveyed with an almost biblical simplicity which is refuted by the un-Christianlike violence with which he assaults his recalcitrant donkey. In the fifth and final opening we are introduced to Jane

Moon at her toilette; the prose is heavily reminiscent of Joyce's parody of women's magazine fiction in the *Nausikaa* section of *Ulysses*. The blushing romanticism reaches a peak before being dismantled: 'She jumped up with a cry wrung out of her heart, tears of joy streaming down her face, and started to run towards his strong brown arms, forgetting that her knickers were round her ankles. She fell heavily on the bathmat, and the tight roll of paper she had been holding on her lap spun away, unwinding itself across the floor' (p. 17).

This fragmented opening to the novel asserts disorder by holding out to the reader the vague promise of order. At the end of the first section a ribbon of white paper unrolls itself across the street as Malquist's coach runs down the fat woman who has hurled the tight roll of paper at the window. The white ribbon appears again as Jane Moon hits the bathroom floor, promising a continuity which is consistently withheld. This sense of emerging pattern is reinforced by the deliberate symmetry formed by the endings of four of the five openings. Jane's fall in the final opening repeats that of Lady Malquist in the third; the Risen Christ's donkey's refusal to move reflects the single-mindedness of Slaughter's mare who dictates her own pace, despite the protestations of the rider. So, Stoppard is deliberately invoking the presence of two orders, employing pattern only to deny it and to assert the impossibility of incarnating a stable viewpoint in a privileged style.

'A book may have three openings entirely dissimilar and inter-related only in the prescience of the author,' (p. 9) claimed O'Brien's student narrator. In *Lord Malquist and Mr Moon* the attempt to relate the fragmented events of the opening in the *hindsight* of a prospective author is one of comic incompetence. At the end of chapter 2, Moon, assailed by the combined pressure of all his old multiplying fears, presses the plunger on the bomb in his pocket. It begins to tick away, an agent of destruction balancing Moon's pained attempts to order what is happening around him. Instantaneously, disorder asserts itself. Moon's notebook, his garbled record of the events of the day, is set alight as it dries out over an electric fire. When Moon attempts his chronicle for January 29th, in the next chapter, his verbal record undergoes a parallel decomposition. The 'author' can establish no transparent transcription of what has occurred.

Moon's chronicle is decked out in the trappings of an eighteenth-century diarist: 'Awoke late as is my custom,' he begins, magisterially, 'and since my wife Jane had been up betimes, breakfasted alone' (p. 92). Moon continues, at first, to maintain this air of efficiency. We hear of his meeting with a handsome gentleman, 'most dramatically dressed in a black cape lined with silk of the palest blue that matched his cravat,' mounted upon a horse that gleamed like coal (p. 94). He tells us, impassively, of the incident in the park in which the gentleman's Tibetan lion hound jumps on the back of a park-keeper. However, as the chronicle moves towards a conclusion events begin to overtake the style; the comings and goings of cowboys and Risen Christ are hurriedly dispensed with: 'Lord Malquist and I went inside,' he says of his arrival home, 'and I was privileged to introduce my wife Jane to him. She was entertaining a friend, Mr Jones, and not long afterwards another gentleman called, also riding a horse. He was acquainted with Mr Jones. Both he and Mr Jones rode off on their horses. Meanwhile a man on a donkey had also stopped outside my house and we welcomed him in to join us' (p. 101). The quickening pace and blurring of detail tell of the confusion threatening to crack the surface of the prose.

In composing his chronicle, Moon 'typed badly and when it came to framing sentences he found that he had no natural style and that it was all coming out stilted' (p. 106). Moon is chronically disabled by that openness of mind celebrated by the protagonist/narrator of *At Swim-Two-Birds:* deprived of a stable position from which he may see the world he can select and sustain no 'natural' style to transcribe it. The sky has been turned into a huge mirror and Moon has seen himself and his fellows unawares.

Moon proclaims himself 'wide-open to things' and confesses to a 'secret knowledge' (p. 18). That secret knowledge is knowledge of the possibility of contradiction; he is wide-open to the contrary assertion which will cancel everything out. ' "I cannot commit myself to either side of a question" ' he explains. ' "Because if you attach yourself to one or the other you disappear into it" ' (p. 54). He says that he takes both parts, ' "leapfrogging along the great moral issues, refuting myself and rebutting the refutation towards a truth which must be the compound of two opposite half-truths" ' (p. 52). Guildenstern's fear is of discovering, or even suspecting, that his spontaneity is part of somebody else's order; Moon's dilemma is defined by a similar need to discover what is truly spontaneous to him – and the fear that such 'natural' behaviour is pure fiction. ' "The thing about people," ' he says, ' "is that hardly anyone behaves naturally any more, they all behave the way they think they are supposed to be, as if they'd read about themselves or seen themselves at the pictures" ' (p. 53). Part of him is convinced that originality has been used up and part of him admits that ' "faith in one's uniqueness dies hard" ' (p. 53).

Moon is constantly startled by the minutiae of everyday life: 'Every response gave Moon the feeling that reality was just outside his perception. If he made a certain move, changed the angle of his existence to the common ground, logic and absurdity would separate. As it was he couldn't pin them down' (p. 32). His world has been radically defamiliarised: he *sees* as absurd what others recognise as logical and natural. His distance from the common ground is measured by his acutely sensitised perception of the world around him: 'For some reason Jane's lips appeared to have been painted pink. He wondered whether the illusion was optical or transcendental. Then he noticed that her eyes were edged with green lines that shaded into the recesses of her lids' (p. 33). What defines the comic pain of his predicament is the fact that perception, for him, is fluctuation. The contrary position asserts itself: 'Its familiarity ambushed him: lipstick and eyeshadow. Once more the commonplace had duped him into seeing absurdity, just as absurdity had tricked him into accepting it as commonplace' (pp. 33–4). Moon rebounds back and forth from the assumptions of the common ground to horrified faith in his own dissent.

The extent of Moon's confusion can be seen in his reaction to a society which, in his eyes, has spun out of control and is heading for disaster. Tensed for the apocalyptic moment, Moon feels that the logic of society remains unimpeachable only because we refuse to take a look at it: 'The technical and human complexity of the machine shook on the very edge of disintegration, held together only by everyone else's unawareness of the fact' (pp. 43–4). 'In a film cartoon,' it is explained, 'when someone runs off the edge of a cliff he goes on running in mid-air for a few yards; only when he looks down and becomes aware does he drop. Moon had looked down and seen the abyss' (p. 44). In other words, like Guildenstern, Moon refuses simply to honour what the Player calls the currency of living. For Moon, the social mechanism has been defamiliarised: he is not content to *recognise* what has simply been taken on trust. Characteristically, he reacts in two opposite ways to his suspicion that the logic underpinning the way we live may be pure illusion. The first is to retreat, to withdraw, to seal himself off against 'his integrality with a vast complex of moving parts all dependent on each other and maintained on the brink of disintegration only by their momentum' (p. 19). His attempts to secure the 'common ground' are also a form of retreat; like the 'Beckett refugee' (in a reflex explored by Beckett in his essay on Proust) Moon constructs a defensive habit to exclude the possibility of disturbing insight – but this defence is constantly broken down: 'He had learned to detach himself, insecurely, and then a word spoken or a figure in a newspaper or a street with cars parked down both sides would rout him all over again' (p. 42).

As the bizarre events in his home begin to get out of hand, 'Moon watched. He was not involved, he was a spectator. It was a private view' (p. 110). However, Moon is quite incapable of maintaining this sense of indifference and detachment, of (to return to the words Stoppard used in *Scene* to describe parallel instances in Muriel Spark's novels) blinking at the 'multitude of aberrations' which 'reveal human absurdity'. A contrary response continually asserts itself, and when it does Moon is not content with cultivating the attitude of the disinterested spectator; he addresses himself to the task of ambushing everyone else, of shocking them into acknowledging the spectacle of disorder. Moon explains to the uncomprehending Long John Slaughter that he needs a bomb for precisely this purpose: ' "we require an explosion. It is not simply a matter of retribution, it is a matter of shocking people into a moment of recognition – *bang!* – so that they might make a total reassessment, recognise that life has gone badly wrong somewhere." ' Slaughter pulls reflectively on his lower lip and then, indicating the typewriter and sheets of paper, asks, innocently, ' "Are you some kind of a writer?" ' (p. 116).

Lord Malquist, of course, suffers none of Moon's pained and comic vacillation. Having announced his intention to withdraw with style from the chaos, he aspires to the detachment which Moon can only maintain intermittently. He proclaims a change in the heroic posture from that of the man of action ' "to that of the Stylist, the spectator as hero, the man of inaction who would not dare roll up his sleeves for fear of creasing the cuffs" ' (p. 79). He acknowledges that such detachment is a form of retreat and, as his creditors close around him, confides that he has nowhere to retreat to any more: ' "I have withdrawn from a number of positions and made my stand anew with my diminished resources drawn in around me . . . but now I am at a loss" ' (p. 187). Resigning himself to his fate as a martyr to the cause of hereditary privilege, Malquist, disdaining to outlive his wealth, lives a life of elegant suicide. ' "Let it be said of me" ' he announces from his bath, ' "that I was born appalled, lived disaffected, and died in the height of fashion" ' (p. 189).

The submerged debate about the nature and pretensions of art restates the basic conflict between the yearnings of Moon and the protective indifference of the ninth earl. Art, for Malquist, is Style: ' "an aesthetic inbred and disengaged" ' (p. 79). He confides to his hired Boswell that he too has pretensions to being a writer and, allowing that he would rather his book were unread than ungraceful, explains that he is writing a monograph on *Hamlet* as a source of book-titles, ' "a subject which does not interest me in the slightest, but I would like to leave behind me one slim and useless volume bound in calf and marked with a ribbon" ' (pp. 67–8). Style is the distance by which form has disengaged itself from content. Malquist compounds his musings on the status of literature by pointing to the example of Carlyle. He tries to comfort Moon with the knowledge that Carlyle too suffered from the 'saving grace' of impotence and goes on to recall his remark: ' "I do not pretend to understand the universe. It is a great deal bigger than I am" ' (p. 186). Malquist holds up Carlyle as the archetypal literary artist who celebrates man's inability to deal with the problematic except by ignoring it, seeking compensation in the fixity and refuge of artistic form. Substance, insists Malquist, is ephemeral, but style is eternal: ' "which may not be a solution to the realities of life but it is a workable alternative" ' (p. 156).

Malquist claims that he stands for style, and that there is nothing else. '*There is everything else*,' insists Moon, silently. '*Substance. I stand for substance*' (p. 63). Moon falls immediately into his own trap, finding himself unable to define the substance of his own remark: 'That wasn't true at all, he didn't even know what it meant' (p. 63). Despite this instant and reflexive disclaimer, it is clear that Moon attempts to counter Malquist's aesthetics of disengagement with his own version of an aesthetics of engagement. Malquist expects the writer to ignore the problematic; Moon, however, 'was trying to frame a question that would take in all the questions, and elicit an answer that would be all the answers' (p. 30). In other words, Moon (to return to the terms in which Chekhov frames the matter) sees the obligation of the artist as the providing of not just the correct setting of a problem, but the correct *solution* of the problem. Unfortunately, this self-imposed task is palpably beyond him; Moon can find neither the certainty he yearns for, nor that privileged discourse which will fix that certainty in words. He talks of the problem in the adopted idiom of Prufrock (demonstrating, again, that a style does not present itself 'naturally' to him): 'when I've got it in a formulated phrase, when I've got it formulated, sprawling on a pin, when it is pinned and wriggling on the wall, then how should I begin . . . ?' (p. 24). Of course, the crux of his predicament is that he *cannot* begin; he has yet to embark on his history of the world because he cannot put down a word without suspecting that it is the wrong one and continually holds back for another day in the hope that the intervening experience will provide the right one: 'Moon fearfully glimpsed himself as a pure writer who after a lifetime of absolutely no output whatsoever, would prepare on his deathbed the single sentence that was the distillation of every-thing he had saved up, and die before he was able to utter it' (p. 29).

The irony is clear: as a writer Moon is as 'sterile' as Malquist. In the final analysis, he can only 'engage' with problems by trying to blow them away. The bomb is his admission of failure: his search for certainty and order and its permanent fixity in language will culminate, he decides, in the bringing of destruction: 'he had a bomb and the bomb promised purgation. He would be presumptuous' (p. 24). Moon's position is, then, cancelled as effectively as that of Malquist, who chooses the moment when his coach gallops the wrong way into the oncoming traffic to announce, amid the ensuing frag-mentation of glass and steel, that he recoils from such chaos, from this ' "utter disregard for the common harmonies of life" ' (p. 21).

The opposing views on the nature of art held by Moon and Malquist echo those Stoppard had found in *Next Time I'll Sing To You* and had already used in *Rosencrantz and Guildenstern are Dead*. Malquist expects art to disengage itself from disorder, to deign to reflect nothing. Moon, on the other hand, sees art as revelatory: an ordered microcosm *reflecting* and uncovering the order in the macrocosm. Stoppard, however, invokes in his novel the analogy of art-as-mirror to introduce a third term which refuses the stark alternatives presented by Malquist and Moon and which suggests something about his own art. Moon enters Marie's bedroom; the maid lies dead beneath the chesterfield downstairs, shot by a cowboy, and Moon catches himself in her mirror: 'his compassion for his image was reflected back into himself but it did not comfort him. When he leaned forward between the hinged mirror-leaves he caught the reflection of his reflection and the reflection of that, and of that, and he saw himself multiplied and diminished between the mirrors, himself aghast in the exact centre of a line that stretched to the edges of a flat earth. He closed his eyes and got up and fell over the dressing-stool' (p. 87). If Stoppard's art is a mirror, it too has hinged leaves and, like Moon, upon looking into it, we see reflections of reflections – ourselves multiplied by our own attempts to interpret and give shape to the lives we lead. The image helps to cast an ironic reflection on Wardle's disapproving description of Stoppard's plays as 'looking-glass adventures'.

It transpires that Moon's episode with Lady Malquist, which he sees as the focal point around which his life will assume order and significance, is just such a looking-glass adventure. On his way to her bedroom he takes a wrong turning; he opens a pair of large double doors painted cream with gilt mouldings and, through the gap, sees himself 'looking at himself through a gap in a large pair of double doors painted lilac' (p. 134). Moon finally bumps into Laura Malquist and follows her into the bedroom, 'which was large and white, gilt-trimmed, lemon-draped, and dominated by a four-poster bed, which, white, gilded and draped, seemed like a miniature of the room itself' (p. 135). The looking-glass adventure unrolls in exactly the way that Wardle describes: Stoppard establishes a contrast between the world of artifice (the mirrored reflection and the miniature double) and the world of the 'real' (Moon's emotions) and then, as he moves on to describe the seduction, negates it.

Moon's first experience of sex is far from the raw exposure to the 'real' that he imagines it to be. Laura leans back against him and he 'allowed her neck to excite him through his fingertips, watching her face in the mirror' (p. 141). The significance of the reference to the mirror is made explicit by Moon's later explanation of why he and Jane are still virgins: ' "I didn't go about it the right way, we never got into the frame of mind where it became natural, we kept pretending to be natural but really we were watching ourselves being natural, and she couldn't" ' (pp. 142–3). Moon is saved the embarrassment of deciding what would be the natural thing to do because it is Lady Malquist who takes the initiative, 'like an ondine beguiling a drowned sailor into her cave' (p. 143). The description of Laura turning under him with underwater grace and making sea-moans that lingered in the flooded chambers of his mind is transposed, of course, from Prufrock's sexual fantasies. In other words, Stoppard is completing the equation of artifice: the 'naturalness' of Moon's actions is denied, and his 'real' world is subsumed under that of Eliot's art.

Ironically, Moon, in his moment of greatest euphoria, convinced that the fragments of his life have suddenly slotted into place, finds that he still cannot formulate in a single phrase his post-coital *joie de vivre:* he can still find no 'natural' style to fix and place what has happened to him. He sits up in the bed, a man of experience: *'I've had it away,* he thought, amazed,' pondering how many times a day he will need his sexual fix with Laura, *'I have lain with Lady Malquist (how poetical!). Tupped her* bragged Moon Jacobean, *been intimate with her* claimed Moon journalistic, *I've committed misconduct* admitted Moon co-respondent, *had carnal knowledge* swore Moon legalistic, *in the biblical sense have I known her – I've had an affair with Laura Malquist (O sophisticated Moon!)'* (p. 145). He swings his feet exultantly over the side of the bed and slashes his remaining unwounded foot on a piece of broken whisky bottle. Ironically, Moon re-embarks on his path of painful and unwitting self-laceration at precisely that moment in which he is able, for the first time, to *celebrate* a multiplicity of viewpoint and expression instead of recoiling from it in dismay. Stoppard has handled the whole episode with characteristic care, neatly balancing Moon's belief in the spontaneity and 'naturalness' of his actions with his own preoccupation with those shared and conditioning forms of self-realisation from which he cannot free himself. This, then, is Formalist art as a hinged mirror, showing us Moon as a series of reflections in mirrors both literal and metaphorical.

Moon's experience of the power of stereotypes is another looking-glass adventure. It begins in the bizarre altercation between Malquist's coachman, O'Hara, and the Risen Christ, which is framed as a clash between stage-Jewish and stage-Irish in which O'Hara launches into an anti-Semitic outburst couched in Music-Hall Yiddish. Moon is thrown by this equation which fails to add up; recognisable tokens of normality combine only to increase his sense of absurdity. His confusion with O'Hara reaches a peak a little later when he catches sight of his face just as the streetlights ignite themselves, suggesting 'a *ping* too high for the human ear' as pink filament 'infused their waxen coldness with the promise of light' (p. 49). This is the moment of defamiliarisation: the banality of the streetlights is itself made strange and in their 'unnatural' light Moon is presented with the possibility of 'seeing'. What he sees is that O'Hara's face is 'broad, negroid, black': 'He tried to remember when he had last seen O'Hara, whether he had seen him at all. He had got from somewhere a mental image of O'Hara's face – Irish, boozy and fat. Had he made it up? For the hundredth time in his short memory another trick had been played on him' (pp. 49–50). The stereotype that Moon had constructed – O'Hara as the boozy, fat Irishman – is dissolved, but what he 'sees' in its place is just another stereotype. Again the equation of artifice is completed. Overwhelmed with panic, Moon reels away to surer ground and launches into a vitriolic attack against the stereotyped 'nigger': ' "get back to the jungle and leave our women alone" ' (p. 52). Spent, Moon crawls into the dark of the coach and huddles on the floor. The lachrymose retreat makes explicit the nature of his frightened outburst: his stereotyped reaction to a stereotype is a withdrawal from uncertainty to seek fixity in the surer common ground.

The point is clear: in Moon's looking-glass adventure one stereotype succeeds another and everything is cancelled out; his everyday experience is composed according to the same principle to which Stoppard adheres in opening his novel – as one style cancels another. Indeed, *Lord Malquist and Mr Moon* ends with a deliberate and detailed demonstration of that principle. On his way out of Lord Malquist's home (in which Laura has recently seduced the Risen Christ in the hope of getting pregnant, and the ninth earl is preparing himself for martyrdom), Moon picks up one of Malquist's silver-topped walking sticks and dons one of his cloaks and hats. He takes an undignified tumble down the steps, but is bundled into the malquist by O'Hara and manages to recover himself sufficiently to strike the authentic Malquistian tone. We are then given a mirror-image of the opening of the novel as the coach rocks up the road to the corner of Birdcage Walk. Instead of the fat woman hurling the petition against the window of Malquist's coach, 'the man with the bowler hat and the long sad moustache jumped out from under a tree and threw something which smashed the glass in the coach window and landed heavily in Moon's lap' (p. 192). This, of course, is the husband of the woman run down at the beginning by Malquist, and he is seeking retribution with a bomb. Moon 'caught the look of apologetic concern on Mr Cuttle's face just before the coach blew up. The horses bolted again, dispersing Moon and O'Hara and bits of pink and yellow wreckage at various points along the road between the Palace and Parliament Square' (p. 192). Moon is destroyed, mistaken for his spiritual adversary. In recognising Cuttle, of course, he sees himself also; the anarchist's attempt to revenge himself on Malquist misfires as disastrously as would have Moon's attempt to champion the principle of order had his bomb been real. In other words, a double cancellation has taken place: Moon's sense of his own uniqueness is cancelled out by a negating of the difference between himself and both Malquist and the anarchist.[10]

Stoppard, then, follows O'Brien and *At Swim-Two-Birds* in making use of a central character who suffers from a chronic 'openness of mind' (refusing to rest easy in those conventions which constitute the currency of living for those around him) to deny the tenets of realism. However, Stoppard departs from O'Brien's approach by creating, in Moon himself, something of an apologist for realism; as a would-be writer Moon condemns himself to a vain search for a quintessential style which will replace the self-evident shams in which everyone else is prepared to invest (and in exploiting which O'Brien's narrator so gleefully delights). In essence, it is by engaging with Moon's yearning for fixity and a privileged transcription of reality (denying his sense of the stability of his own ego, countering style with style) that Stoppard's novel frees itself from the constraints those terms imply. Although discredited as a spokesman, Moon is valuable, nevertheless, because of his direct and painful experience of the breakdown of habitual, mechanised perception. That breakdown, of course, is identified by the Formalist critic as the function of literariness and becomes the strategic goal of Stoppard in his Theatre of Formalism.

4

A Theatre of Formalism

I

'I used to feel out on a limb,' admits Stoppard, 'because when I started to write you were a shit if you weren't writing about Vietnam or housing. Now I have no compunction about that . . . *The Importance of Being Earnest* is important, but it says nothing about anything.'[1] As we shall see later, in *Travesties* Stoppard the playwright pinpoints what Wilde was up to with rather more accuracy than this overstatement allows; nevertheless, the remark deserves our attention. Stoppard's championing of a drama which says nothing about anything is not simply a new aestheticism, 'a delectation,' in Eichenbaum's words, 'with certain elements of form consciously divorced from "content" '.[2] It is, rather, an elevation of form to the status of content. His plays evoke the two orders (preservation of the traditional canon and deviation from that canon) and in so doing they perform a critical function – speaking of those procedures which have brought them into being, and with which they so clamorously argue.

Stoppard, according to Brian Crossley, is ever the theatrical critic, the parodic and self-referential quality of his work setting him apart from the 'Juvenalian' writers of the previous generation. His criticism, continues Crossley, is aimed at the mores of drama, and especially at the age-old detective-figure of Sophocles' Oedipus. The main thrust of Stoppard's aesthetic attack is to turn this tradition against itself.[3] Crossley is overstating his case, of course; the detective-figure and the whodunnit-form of which he is a part combine as just one of the targets for Stoppard's parodic strategies. It is, however, a particularly useful one, presupposing as it does an investigation brought to a successful conclusion, a question emphatically answered. In Stoppard's hands the whodunnit is nudged into unfamiliar outline. By means of that act of defamiliarisation Stoppard's own drama distances itself from the supposition that its proper end (echoes of Chekhov again here) is the offering of solutions, the undertaking of an investigation in which the truth will out.

The Real Inspector Hound is, of course, the most obvious example of Stoppard's parodic engagement with the whodunnit. The most enthusiastic notices for the original 1968 production came from Ronald Bryden in *The Observer* who found it 'nearly perfect in its kind' and thanked heaven for a new comic master. Unfortunately, Bryden, in his ecstasy, misunderstands the play. He speaks of theatricality closing about the critics Moon and Birdboot as they become caught up by the action on stage: 'They have fallen out of the world into a mad, revolving cage of artifice.' What we witness, then, is 'someone else swallowed up by the universal nightmare of slipping out of ordered experience into chaos'.[4] This, quite demonstrably, is not what happens in *The Real Inspector Hound*. In the first instance, Moon and Birdboot do not fall into a world of chaos but into a world of palpable order. Second, as Irving Wardle notes, *The Real Inspector Hound* completes an equation of artifice: the apparent contrast between the action of the spoofed thriller and the lives of the critics in the stalls is established only to be negated. As Michael Billington says, in a review of the play directed by Stoppard in a double-bill with Sheridan's *The Critic*, the effect is of *parallel* worlds colliding.[5] What this amounts to is an assault on the audience's sense of superiority towards the parodied stage-action, a questioning of those fixed categories of illusion and actuality with which Stoppard is, apparently, inviting us to judge it.

'*The first thing*,' reads the published text of the play, '*is that the audience appear to be confronted by their own reflection in a huge mirror.*'[6] This initial impression is deceptive in the sense that if Stoppard's play is a mirror it has *hinged* leaves. Although the audience see themselves reflected in the persons of Moon and Birdboot, the two critics will, finally, be seen as reflections of the characters in the play they are reviewing. The same thing happens to the audience as happens to Moon when he peers at himself in the hinged mirror: the audience catch their reflection in the mirror that is Moon and Birdboot reflected in the mirror of Muldoon Manor. This 'hall-of-mirrors' effect criticises that simple model which places art as a reflecting mirror opposite the actuality of life; what is reflected instead is the degree to which life seizes upon the forms of art as a means to self-realisation: reflections, in other words.

In *The Real Inspector Hound* Stoppard's parodic engagement with the whodunnit is most obvious in his use of compression; techniques are defamiliarised by the new context in which they are being repeated and they buckle beneath the pressure of the amount of work they must do. A case in point is the use of Mrs Drudge's answering of the telephone to set the scene by conveying information, apparently indirectly, to the audience. 'Hello,' she cries, greedily snatching up the receiver after an embarrassed pause in which she has dusted it with intense concentration, 'the drawing-room of Lady Muldoon's country residence one morning in early spring?' (p. 15). Having established dramatic place, she obligingly begins to unfold the plot: 'I hope nothing is amiss for we, that is Lady Muldoon and her houseguests, are here cut off from the world, including Magnus, the wheelchair-ridden half-brother of her ladyship's husband Lord Albert Muldoon who ten years ago went out for a walk on the cliffs and was never seen again' (p. 15). In the second act, compression takes further toll and the device is laid hilariously bare: 'The same,' she says into the telephone as the set reillumines about her, 'half an hour later?' (p. 28). The dialogue is so laden with information for the audience in the cause of further uncovering the plot that when it has none to convey and aspires to a form of domestic naturalism, it simply evaporates – as in the scene in which Mrs Drudge works her way around the room offering coffee, milk, sugar and biscuits to, in turn, Cynthia, Felicity and Magnus. 'The second act,' writes Birdboot elaborately in his notebook as the scene threatens to spiral ever onward, 'however, fails to fulfill the promise . . .' (p. 29).

The stage-action is further thrown into relief by the critical pronouncements of Moon and Birdboot in the semi-dark of the mock-auditorium. These remarks are calculated to double-effect. First, the parodied critical observations complete the distinctive Stoppardian mirror-effect: the reflections of Moon and Birdboot *on* the thriller are, in fact, simply reflections *of* it, mechanical and habitual. Second, they ensure a constant rhythm of assertion and refutation as the inanities of Birdboot are juxtaposed with the insistent sententiousness of Moon. 'Me and the lads,' whispers Birdboot as he takes his place alongside Moon, 'have had a meeting in the bar and decided it's first-class family entertainment but if it goes on beyond half-past ten it's self-indulgent – pass it on . . .' (p. 10). 'It's a sort of *thriller*, isn't it?' he asks Moon, who reacts with magisterial aloofness; 'I suppose so. Underneath.' Birdboot is astonished: '*Underneath?!?* It's a whodunnit, man! – Look at it!' (p. 11). This conflict of idioms is maintained throughout. Birdboot is content to take everything at face value: 'A rattling good evening out. I was held' (p. 36), he announces, giving thanks 'and double thanks for a good clean show without a trace of smut' (p. 35). Moon, on the other hand, is determined to wring every last drop of metaphysical significance from the proceedings. 'Faced with such ubiquitous obliquity,' he confesses, 'it is hard, it is hard indeed, and therefore I will not attempt, to refrain from invoking the names of Kafka, Sartre, Shakespeare, St. Paul, Beckett, Birkett, Pinero, Pirandello, Dante and Dorothy L. Sayers' (p. 36). The two parodies (of Birdboot's tabloid commonsense and Moon's upmarket intellectualism) cancel each other out. The point is clear: Moon's responses are no more valid than Birdboot's and both are serenely habitual, the mechanical reduplication of formulae as tired as those which constitute the play they are reviewing.

Moon's remarks, however, supply *The Real Inspector Hound* with a further dimension. Bryden suggested that the two critics are really 'plain-clothes versions of the hapless lords-attendant of Elsinore' and that the play, as a whole, is essentially a parody of Stoppard's own *Rosencrantz and Guildenstern are Dead.*[7] Indeed, Moon and Birdboot are, like Guildenstern and his companion, called upon to unravel and interpret an action which, finally, embraces them with fatal efficiency. For Moon, as for Guildenstern, this investigation into the nature and meaning of what takes place before and around him involves an attempt to establish his own identity. What Bryden does not see, however, in pointing out how *The Real Inspector Hound* burlesques the earlier play, is the way that it cancels its own content. In essence, the play pre-empts its interpretive critics by parodying, through Moon's interjections, the theme of the problematic nature of identity. Once again Stoppard's comments in *Scene* shed light on his practice as a playwright. What he says of Muriel Spark's novels is true of *The Real Inspector Hound:* it does not attempt to prove or promulgate a thesis, it has fun with its premise, plays with it.

Moon, it is quickly established, is obsessed with the figure of Higgs, the regular critic for whom he is deputising. 'It is as if we only existed one at a time,' he complains, 'combining to achieve continuity. I keep space warm for Higgs. My presence defines his absence, his absence confirms my presence, his presence precludes mine' (p. 10). As with his namesake in Stoppard's novel, Moon's faith in his own uniqueness dies hard, despite his fear or suspicion that his identity is defined by Higgs. He insists that there must be something self-sustaining to identify: 'It is merely that it is not enough to wax at another's wane' (p. 19). Inevitably, Moon's brooding on his relationship to Higgs leads him to consider that of Puckeridge, the third-string critic, to himself: 'Does he wait for Higgs and I to write each other's obituary . . . ?' (p. 18). In one important exchange Moon's obsessions overlap with what is happening in the melodrama of Muldoon Manor. 'Higgs,' he murmurs, 'never gives me a second thought, I can tell by the way he nods.' Birdboot, meanwhile, nods knowingly at the familiar pattern of alarums and excursions:

> BIRDBOOT: Revenge, of course.
> MOON: What?
> BIRDBOOT: Jealousy.
> MOON: Nonsense – there's nothing *personal* in it –
> BIRDBOOT: The paranoid grudge –
>
> (p. 19)

The point is well-made: Moon's faith in his own uniqueness and his antipathy to those who threaten it is reflected in (and is, indeed, a reflection of) the formulaic conflicts between the cardboard characters on stage. Moon's reality, the self-sustaining identity he seeks to assert, is negated by the equation of artifice.

It is not only the contrast between Moon and the world of the players that is negated – so is that between Moon's private and public voices. His desire to get 'underneath' the thriller is undertaken with a comic excess of interpretive zeal. He notes, for instance, the classic impact of the catalystic figure setting up shock waves 'which unless I am much mistaken, will strip these comfortable people – these crustaceans in the rock pool of society – strip them of their shells and leave them exposed as the trembling raw meat which, at heart, is all of us' (p. 19). There is, as Wardle points out, no difference between Moon's fabricated private feelings and his parodied critical pronouncements.[8] Stoppard's parody, in effect, exposes the conventional bases of Moon's private anguish. He insists that the whodunnit is really concerned with the problem of identity: 'I think we are entitled to ask – and here one is irresistibly reminded of Voltaire's cry *"Voila!"* – I think we are entitled to ask – *Where is God?*' (p. 28). Moon's susceptibility to the high-sounding cliché denies the very self-sufficiency for which he yearns. As the thriller moves towards its melodramatic climax the semantic collusion of Moon and Birdboot with the world of cheap stereotype is given concrete, dramatic form. Caught on stage, Birdboot finds himself thrust into the sexual imbroglios of Simon Gascoyne – which reflect his own philandering with the actresses offstage. As Moon too is enveloped by the action he turns to find that the equation of artifice has been completed by Hound and Gascoyne, who have occupied his and Birdboot's seats. 'All right,' he yells, assuming the role of the Inspector, galvanised by his grief for Birdboot, 'I'm going to find out who did this!' (p. 45). His search for the identity of Birdboot's killer mirrors, of course, his previous concern as a critic 'with what I have referred to else-where as the nature of identity' (p. 19). In the final scene mask after mask is stripped away. Moon dies recognising Puckeridge playing Albert playing the *real* Inspector playing Magnus Muldoon. With a touch of admiration he realises that the third-string critic has disposed of both himself and Higgs, the body under the sofa. In the final irony he realises that Birdboot had seen through the plot and tried to warn him. Like 'Who Killed Peter Saunders?' it *was* one of those plays, after all.

The Real Inspector Hound, then, is constructed according to that principle of composition so characteristic of Stoppard (and which Stoppard himself identifies as 'Beckettian'). The play establishes a series of oppositions which cancel each other: the opposition between Moon and Birdboot, between Moon's public and private voices, between the two critics and the play they are reviewing. This is not simply a satirical exposé of the inanities of 'Christielised' melo-drama.[9] We are offered no stable viewpoint, no uncountered or destructured position from which the tired formulae of the whodunnit can be seen as any more ridiculous than those which are being used to judge it. We are even denied a meta-language with which we can describe *The Real Inspector Hound* as a whole. Moon's ludicrous minings for metaphysical ore parody and disqualify our own attempts to discuss the play as a serious investigation into the nature of identity. Our position as critics scrutinising 'content' is effectively countered and denied by the comic spectacle of what we presume is Moon's incompetence. We laugh at our own reflection reflected in the palpable distortions of the thriller as the play's self-cancelling oppositions duplicate the form and effect of what Stoppard sees as Beckett's distinctive humour.

The joke, in other words, is on us. When Moon takes over the role of the Inspector he begins to play onstage the part he has been performing off, hounding the moribund thriller to confess its real meaning. He does not bring to this task, however, the clear-eyed perspicacity we might expect. The plot simply overwhelms him. The accusation is clear: we, as critics, are accused of being insufficiently critical about those forms we employ as we *recognise* and order what is happening around us. Birdboot's injunction to simply 'look' at the thriller goes unheeded by Moon. Indeed Moon cannot just 'look' at it; all experience is organised for him by habit 'on labour-saving principles' (to borrow a phrase from Beckett's remarks on Proust[10]). That is to say, his responses and his perceptions are 'enformed' by his obsession with the problem of identity. In this context, *The Real Inspector Hound* can be seen as a comic playing with Shklovsky's distinction between *recognising* and *seeing*. The confusions of *The Real Inspector Hound* are carefully engineered to a demonstrable end: to defamiliarise not just the hackneyed mechanism of the whodunnit but also those habitual categories by means of which we, as critics, might be tempted to recognise it.

In *After Magritte* Stoppard again engages with the whodunnit to uncover the mechanistic and habitual nature of our attempts to make sense of and order the world. The play is constructed out of various attempts to account for and interpret two mysterious sights: the bizarre tableau with which the play opens (and which Inspector Foot regards as 'suspicious') and the apparently unidentifiable witness who will prove the innocence of Harris *et al*. Another Harris, Wendell V., attempts some detective work of his own in *The Explicator*, suggesting that the opening tableau derives from Magritte's painting *L'assassin ménace*.[11] Stoppard may, indeed, have borrowed elements of this design, but Harris is guilty of failing to point out that the effect created by Magritte's painting is entirely and significantly different. In *Scene* Stoppard noted that David Rudkin's *Afore Night Come* was Pinteresque in the way that it explained little or nothing; James Saunders, on the other hand, 'explains little or everything'.[12] In this context the same distinction can be made between Magritte and Stoppard. The painter builds an atmosphere of tension and menace by explaining little or nothing; by explaining little or everything, on the other hand, the dramatist creates a comic effect by offering rival explanations which cancel each other out in the sense of simply compounding confusion.

Harris and his wife are locked in debate about the 'bizarre and desperate figure'[13] they have seen in Ponsonby Place. Thelma recalls a footballer in strip and Harris a pyjama-clad individual carrying not a football but a tortoise. 'You must be blind,' insists Thelma. 'It was he who was blind,' comes the equable response (p. 14). 'I happened to see him with my own eyes,' continues Harris. 'We all saw – '

counters Thelma. 'I am only telling you what I saw!' repeats her husband (p. 19), with mounting fury. Both are adamant that they are only reporting what they have seen; they are also equally incapable of appreciating the degree to which they are not simply passive witnesses but agents of the mystery, burying the initial visual impression deeper and deeper beneath their mutual insistence that every element should cohere and be related to a single explanatory factor. What they discover, in the course of their clash with Foot of the Yard, is that language is as difficult to interpret, as capable of transformation, as the evidence of their senses.

Stoppard's point about puns, claims Clive James, 'isn't so much that the one sound contains multiple meanings, as that it has a different meaning in different places . . . he is at his strongest when one precise meaning is transformed into another precise meaning with the context full-blown in each case.'[14] Such puns pullulate in the dialogue of *After Magritte*. Each speaker attempts to fix their viewpoint in language; the ambiguities which arise through the clash of contexts do so because each explanation of events is countered. 'Meaning', in effect, becomes a battleground for speaker and listener. Foot, for instance, meets Harris' claim that there is a perfectly logical reason for everything apparently untoward in his house with the impassioned rejoinder: 'There is, and I mean to make it stick!' (p. 32). Foot is convinced that 'within the last hour in this room you performed without anaesthetic an illegal operation on a bald nigger minstrel about five-foot-two or Pakistani' (p. 31) and, reminding P.C. Holmes that 'What we're looking for is a darkie short of a leg or two' (p. 33), he meets head-on each protestation to the contrary. 'Is it all right for me to practice?' asks Mother:

> FOOT: No, it is not all right! Ministry standards may be lax but we draw the line at Home Surgery to bring in the little luxuries of life.
> MOTHER: I only practice on the tuba.
> FOOT: Tuba, femur, fibula – it takes more than a penchant for rubber gloves to get a licence nowadays.
>
> (p. 33)

Earlier, Thelma, insisting that the mysterious hopping witness was in fact a West Bromwich Albion footballer, 'carrying under his arm, if not a football then something very similar like a wineskin or a pair of bagpipes,' claims that what he had on his face '*was definitely shaving foam!* (*Pause*) Or possibly some kind of yashmak.' Harris, predictably, will have none of this:

HARRIS: The most – *the very most* – I am prepared to concede
      is that he may have been a sort of street arab making off with
      his lute – *but young he was not and white-bearded he was!*
THELMA: His *loot?*
HARRIS: (*expansively*) Or his mandolin – Who's to say?
                                                          (p. 20)

Stoppard, equally predictably, will not let the pun rest and Foot himself pounces on the word later when Harris suggests that the blind man may have picked up a tortoise in mistake for some other object 'such as a lute' (p. 40).

As in *Artist Descending a Staircase* the whodunnit form of *After Magritte* is parodied and 'made strange' by the simple device of revealing that no crime has, 'in reality', been committed. Foot has set himself a non-existent problem to solve; in so doing, the detective emerges not as the bringer of truth but as the agent of confusion. His insistent search for evidence to substantiate his hypothesis about the supposed double-crime (the robbery among the Victoria Palace Happy Minstrel Troupe and the unlicenced surgery at Mafeking Villas) has brought linguistic confusion to the dialogue of the play, and his guilt is made explicit with the revelation that *he* was the bizarre figure who occasions so much dissension between Thelma and Harris. Like Moon in *The Real Inspector Hound*, Foot is implicated in the mess he is trying to sort out. In both cases Stoppard defamiliarises the whodunnit by 'shifting the dominant': the central element in each play is not the crime and its solution but the *ineptitude* of the methods of detection used by Police Inspector and critic alike. (In *After Magritte* this shifting of the dominant disrupts the internal order of the play in such a way as to negate the contrast between felon and law-enforcer.) The manner of Stoppard's exploitation of and departure from conventional form is significant and, indeed, symptomatic. Once again the particular instances of *The Real Inspector Hound* and *After Magritte* reflect the general case: Stoppard's drama does not set out to offer answers, but to examine the questionable ways we provide them in literary practice. Such an undertaking is an elevation of dramatic form to the status of content and perhaps (to pursue the notion of a shifting dominant) a *displacement* of content by form.

In *Jumpers* a crime – a murder – *has* been committed and the play is Stoppard's most important and inventive use of the whodunnit. As in the two earlier plays Stoppard engages with the audience's expectations of established form – this time by means of a strategic mixing of genres. An examination of the relationship between *Jumpers* and the television drama *Another Moon Called Earth*, upon which it is based, shows how Stoppard uses the whodunnit and a kaleidoscopic array of other dramatic forms to construct a work variously described as 'a perfect, comic, verbal mobile' and, less flatteringly, as a 'paper gazebo'.[15]

Another Moon Called Earth was broadcast live by the BBC in June 1967. 'It seemed to me,' wrote George Melly in *The Observer*, 'rather pretentious.' He dismissed it as an improbable fable but noted that Stoppard himself turned up later on *Late Night Line-Up* and seemed 'very modest, sensible, and clearly talented, even taking R&G into account. Just an off day, perhaps?'[16] To a certain extent, Melly's misgivings are justified. Penelope, the forerunner of Dotty in *Jumpers*, strives painfully to articulate her sense that the moon-landing has marked a traumatic turning-point in man's apprehension of his place in the universe, but Stoppard is unable to create for her a language sufficiently pliant to express her feelings of spiritual dislocation. Instead he settles for a clumsy and clogged sententiousness. 'He stood off the world with his feet on solid ground,' says Penelope of the 'moon man', 'and brought everything into question – because up till then the world was all there was – and always had been – it was us and we were it – and every assumption was part of the world which was all there was, and is no longer – '.[17] It is hard to overcome the suspicion that Penelope's struggle is here shared by Stoppard. In fact, the development of a language for Dorothy in *Jumpers* which can express a sense of collapse and dissolution without succumbing to it is symptomatic of the essential difference between this and the stage play which grew from it.

In *Another Moon Called Earth* the murder to be solved is that of Pinkerton, Penelope's maid (and former nanny), who is pushed from a window overlooking a celebratory parade for the return of the lunanaut. Stoppard has said of Darwin and his revelation in the Galapagos that 'When the idea that it was the *islands* which had made the creatures the way they were, struggled into his consciousness, it was like "confessing a murder".'[18] Penelope commits (and confesses to) a murder because a similar thought has struggled into her consciousness: that the Earth is not at the centre of a benign God's plan. The moon-landing has effected a thoroughgoing dislocation of perspective. 'There goes God in his golden capsule,' she cries, as the lunanaut passes in triumph. 'You'd think that he was sane, to look at him, but he doesn't smile because he has seen the whole thing for what it is – not the be-all and end-all any more, but just another moon called Earth – part of the works and no rights to say what really goes – he's made it all random' (p. 108). Penelope, then, anticipates Dotty in reacting hysterically to the nudging into outline of those familiar truths upon which they have been accustomed to base their lives (as Penelope puts it: 'suddenly everything we live by – our rules – our good, our evil – our ideas of love, duty – all the things we've counted on as being absolute truths – because we filled all existence – they're all suddenly exposed as nothing more than local customs' (p. 99)). In this moment of defamiliarisation (of shifting perspective) the absolute is seen as merely the product of a shared mechanism of public self-defence – as the currency of living, the creation of habit.

In direct contrast to the emotionalism of Penelope is her husband's cold logic. Bone's obsession with logic has led him, like Mr Moon, to devote his life to writing a history of the world, to 'lay bare the logic in which other men have taken to be an arbitrary sequence of accidents' (p. 93). Unfortunately, such is the complexity of the grand design that Bone believes he is uncovering that he has so far failed to get beyond the Greeks and the third century BC. However, as with both Moon and George Moore, Bone's capacity for logical thought is constantly being tested by his wife's behaviour. Jane Moon and her admirers – the cowboys and the ninth earl – continually present Moon with what *looks* like evidence of adultery; similarly, Dotty and Archie *appear* to have developed a relationship which transcends the accepted limits of that defining doctor and patient. In *Another Moon Called Earth* Penelope has spent the last ten days in bed, with Albert (Archie's forerunner) making a call every day. 'Do not think you are dealing with a man who has lost his grapes,' boasts Bone. 'Putting two and two together is my speciality' (p. 94). As is also the case with Moon and George Moore, Bone's relationship with his wife encapsulates the peripheral position to which his intellectual obsessions have condemned him. He is both frustrated *voyeur* and (despite solving the riddle of Pinkerton's death) incompetent detective. *Another Moon Called Earth* is, then, founded on a typically Stoppardian series of cancellations. Bone's engagement with the complexities of history is also a withdrawal from the problems of the moment to the abstractions of the study; similarly, Penelope's immersion in the moral confusions of the sublunary here-and-now, equally paradoxically, manifests itself as a withdrawal to the womb-like security of her bed and the 'safety' of children's games (Pinkerton, we learn, has had the temerity to beat her at 'Battleships').

Obviously, *Another Moon Called Earth* shares many of the basic elements of *Jumpers*. The similarities between the two married couples are complemented by those between Sir Archibald Jumper and Albert, who also suffers from what will become known in *Jumpers* as the Cognomen Syndrome. 'My name is Pearce. Albert Pearce,' he announces as Penelope screams hysterically from the bedroom;

PENELOPE: Rape! Rape! Rape!
ALBERT: I believe she's ready for me.
(p. 103)

'Funny thing,' explains Albert, 'I knew a fellow called Bone once – I wonder if he was a relation? Yes, he wanted to be an osteopath but he couldn't face the pleasantries which every patient would have felt obliged to make, so he took his wife's maiden name of Foot and now practices in Frinton as a chiropodist' (pp. 102–3). The joke survives, of course, in *Jumpers* and the story of Bones's brother. However, the varying use it is put to in the two plays is, in fact, symptomatic of the basic difference between them. In *Another Moon Called Earth* the Cognomen Syndrome (although not named as such) is the occasion for a couple of fairly inconsequential jokes. In *Jumpers*, however, it is demonstrably part of the fabric of the play: an example of the compulsions of language which, as we shall see later in discussing the nature and success of George's dissent, produces the comic dilemma of a philosopher with the cognomen Moore. In *Jumpers* language operates as a formal constraint against which George struggles in an attempt to articulate and argue his belief. It is precisely this involution of the problems of belief and form which distinguishes *Jumpers* from *Another Moon Called Earth*. In the television play the thematic concern with shifting perspective (in Penelope's attainment of a lunar viewpoint from which all our truths have edges, and Bone's attempt to decide how to regard his wife's behaviour) dominates the play, preventing its form becoming a subject of attention.

'The attraction of unexpected, unnatural, or "unnaturalistic" things happening on stage,' claims Stoppard, 'is precisely that they *are* happening on a *stage*. The surprising effects depend partly on the audience's barely conscious knowledge of the limitations of the stage. A lot of things I like very much as pieces of staging in *Jumpers* or *Travesties* would be more or less pointless if you were making a movie of either of those plays.'[19] *Jumpers*, like *Travesties*, is theatre of audacity, a series of ambushes for the audience. As this remark suggests, these ambushes work in the same way as he expects humour to: they both gratify and surprise expectations. In effect, the freedom of *Jumpers* emerges from a careful observation of established procedure and discipline – and the freedom of the staging (a troupe of acrobats, a trapeze-artist, the use of a revolving stage and a huge television screen) complements and parallels the play's formal freedom. *Jumpers* enacts a constant dislocation of the audience's perspective by means of a critical engagement with their knowledge of the limitations of genre. This is a dimension which *Another Moon Called Earth* (as a live television broadcast a curious hybrid of stage and film) totally lacks.

'The truth to us philosophers, Mr Crouch,' announces Archie, just before the end of Act 2, 'is always an interim judgment. We will never even know for certain who did shoot McFee. Unlike mystery novels, life does not guarantee a denouement: and if it came, how would one know whether to believe it?'[20] In *Another Moon Called Earth* a denouement is forthcoming: Penelope is clearly the perpetrator of the dastardly crime against poor Pinkers. In *Jumpers*, on the other hand, Dotty is just one of the suspects: the closing moments of Act 2 suggest that George's secretary may well have been the murderer, commiting a crime of passion (even though it soon transpires that the apparently damning splash of blood on her white coat is, in fact, that of George's pet hare), while Archie's summary treatment of the Archbishop of Canterbury, Sam Clegthorpe, in George's dream suggests that he was the murderer, wreaking terrible vengeance for McFee's rather embarrassing apostasy. This final solution to the mystery may seem the most likely, but Stoppard is careful to undercut our certainty. George, after all, has already proved himself a detective at least as incompetent as Inspector Bones. For instance: 'There are many things I know which are not verifiable,' he admits to Archie, 'but nobody can tell me I don't know them, and I think that I know that something happened to poor Dotty and she somehow killed McFee, as sure as she killed my poor Thumper' (p. 78). Dotty, of course, did not kill Thumper, George himself did – impaling the hare upon an arrow fired in an attempt to disprove Zeno. As we shall see, George's mistake is an ironic comment on his own claims to an intuitionist philosophy; in this context, however, its main function is to prevent us from accepting him as a totally reliable interpreter of events. The coda (George's dream) does not simply close the question: it proffers a denouement but asks, as it does so, how we know whether to believe it. In other words, Stoppard defamiliarises the whodunnit by means of a literary short-circuit. *Jumpers* is an example of what Fortunatov calls 'negative form': the play *appears* to move towards a crisis, a moment of closure which will order what has gone before, but which never occurs. The action remains inconclusive and the incompleteness of the whodunnit is a function of *ostranenie*. How the hell, we may ask with George, does one know what to believe?

Of *Travesties* Stoppard has said that he wanted to dislocate the audience's assumptions every now and again about what kind of style the play was going to be in: 'Dislocation of an audience's assumptions is a large part of what I like to write.'[21] Within the overall 'negative form' of the whodunnit, this dislocation is repeatedly effected, in *Jumpers*, by *obnaženie priëma:* the laying bare of a literary device by its repetition in a new and incongruous context. The whodunnit, for instance, itself cancelled and made strange, provides an incongruous backdrop to the theatre of debate between George and the philosophical mainstream. Similarly, the debate-format is itself constantly disrupted by devices borrowed from farce. In the original production, as Stoppard points out in a footnote, George's abstracted peregrinations between study and bedroom were counterpointed by the swinging in and out of view of the dead jumper hooked on the inside of a cupboard door, which, mysteriously, opened upon the closing of the bedroom door: 'a device borrowed from the famous Robert Dhery sketch in *La Plume de ma Tante*' (p. 30). To this specific instance can be added the generic: cross-purpose dialogue, mistaken identity, and the more or less improbable explanations of characters caught in what would appear to be something very like *flagrante delicto*. This recourse to farce and whodunnit amounts to a canonisation of the junior branch – and a critical engagement with the theatre of serious debate. However, Stoppard is careful to use a device from 'quality' literature to prevent either of these popular forms establishing its dominance. In the opening moments of the play a troupe of not-quite proficient acrobats assembles itself bravely into a human pyramid from which one of their number is blown, fatally, by a gunshot from the outer darkness. These apparently inexplicable events (coupled with the spectacular striptease on the trapeze and Dotty's addled rendition of a medley of moon songs) form the mystery that we expect what follows to explain: the crime which sets the whodunnit in motion. Yet a twist to the literary kaleidoscope will give us a different focus. It is possible to regard these opening events as a concrete metaphor for the flashy gymnastics of modern philosophy (and their consequences). Seen in this way, the play opens with a device borrowed from the Absurdist canon. *Jumpers*, however, is not an Absurdist play any more than it is farce, whodunnit or serious debate. It is the argument of form with form, the point where genres join and clash. It does not simply create a dramatic structure from a diversity of materials: it asserts its own freedom by demonstrating and departing from (in essence, *engaging* with) the disciplines and constraints those materials exact.

Jumpers turns to good account that dislocation of perspective which incapacitates Dotty. As the play opens, and the jumpers perform their all too bloody likely acrobatics, Dotty announces her intention to do 'the one about the moon' (p. 19). What follows is her attempt to single out and perform one particular song about the moon from her repertoire. The musicians, we are told, 'attempt to follow her but are thwarted by her inability to distinguish one moon-song and another, and by her habit of singing the words of one to the tune of another' (p. 19). Her act is in ruins; Dotty is routed by the lack of congruence between these songs and her brooding obsession with the portentous events in the lunar wastes. In effect, Dotty's problems with the moon-songs contain in little her problems with expression as a whole. Her new viewpoint is defined by the wreckage of that she has abandoned; consequently, the outburst in which she attains the most powerful expression of her new perspective is, effectively, a critical engagement with the language of the Bible. All our absolutes, she claims, looked like the local customs of another place to the two moonmen with one neck to save between them: 'When that thought drips through to the bottom, people won't just carry on. There is going to be such . . . breakage, such gnashing of unclean meats, such covetting of neighbours' oxen and knowing of neighbours' wives, such dishonourings of mothers and fathers, and bowings and scrapings to images graven and incarnate, such killing of goldfish and maybe more – ' (p. 75). It is the presence, and the breakdown, of Biblical form that constitutes Dotty's voice at this point. The Bible is indeed made strange. For Dotty, this collapse of established form is the catastrophic harbinger of a moral apocalypse from which she retreats into neurosis. On the other hand, as we have seen, it is, for the author of *Jumpers*, a principle of composition.

In fact, it is not just the formal structure but also the very language of the play which is created from the redeployment and laying bare of established and canonised models. Dotty, for instance, looks back to a time before all was called into question and the moon was ~~simply~~ '*Keats's* bloody moon! – for what has made the sage or poet write but the fair paradise of nature's light – And *Milton's* bloody moon! rising in clouded majesty, at length apparent queen, unveiled her peerless light and o'er the dark her silver mantle threw – And Shelley's sodding maiden, with white fire laden, whom mortals call the – (weeping) *Oh yes, things were in place then!*' (p. 41). The classics, fragmented to varying degrees, make similar appearances throughout the text. There is, for instance, an insistent thread of allusion to Shakespeare. 'Oh, horror, horror, horror!' screams Dotty from the bedroom as George has God typed out in the study, 'Confusion now hath made its masterpiece . . . most sacriligious murder! (*Different voice*) Woe, alas! What, in our house?' (p. 24). She is here conflating the words of Macduff, upon discovering the murder of the King, with those of Lady Macbeth, professing her ignorance thereof (see *Macbeth*, II. iii.) – an unseen charade which, incidentally, suggests that she may have had a hand in the murder of McFee, whose christian name happens to be Duncan. There are two further instances of lines from Shakespeare. In the coda Archie wheels on Sam Clegthorpe, who voices his distress at seeing his 'flock' weeping in his garden in Lambeth. 'My Lord Archbishop,' says Archie, 'when I was last in Lambeth I saw good strawberries in your garden – I do beseech you send for some' (p. 85). In so doing, Archie echoes the words of Gloucester to the Bishop of Ely: 'When I was last in Holborn,/I saw good strawberries in your garden there:/I do beseech you send for some of them' (*Richard III*, III.iv.). Gloucester says this moments before ordering the execution of Hastings. This allusion acts as a counterbalance, in other words, to Dotty's identification earlier with Lady Macbeth, suggesting the possibility (or, at least, the dreaming George's suspicion) that it is Archie who is the culprit – ensuring his ascendancy in the same way as Gloucester clinches his coronation. If George sees Archie as Gloucester, at one point he casts himself in the role of Hamlet. As he marches to answer the door, confident that the caller is Archie, he lifts his pet tortoise and whispers into what he hopes is his ear: 'Now might I do it, Pat' (p. 43). The line, of course, is a comic reworking of Hamlet's (III. iii.) when he discovers the unwitting and unattended Claudius at prayer. Yet George is not Prince Hamlet, nor was meant to be. The comic undercutting of the line emphasises his position as a peripheral figure rather than a hero, a position he half acknowledges by means of fragmented quotation from another 'classic' author: T. S. Eliot. 'It was a wet day,' he says, recalling his first meeting with Dotty, 'your hair was wet . . . and I thought, "The hyacinth girl" . . . "How my hair is growing thin" ' (p. 33). In so doing he refers to *The Waste Land* ('The Burial of the Dead') and to *The Love Song of J. Alfred Prufrock*, dramatising himself as Eliot's 'attendant lord'.

These allusions promise a pattern of signification which, in fact, never materialises. Literature, as a point of stable reference, is disrupted – as is history. *Jumpers* rewrites the story of Scott and the heroism of Oates. 'Millions of viewers,' the television tells us, 'saw the two astronauts struggling at the foot of the ladder until Oates was knocked to the ground by his commanding officer. . . . Captain Scott has maintained radio silence since pulling up the ladder and closing the hatch with the remark, "I am going up now. I may be gone for some time" ' (p. 23). Oates's famous words are wrenched from him and inverted by their new context. Similarly, as we shall see later in focusing on the involution of the academic philosophical material and the rest of the play, the *historical* George Moore, the Cambridge philospher, receives comparable treatment. Stoppard and *Jumpers* make free with the disciplines of history, questioning the significance we have attributed to it, and the configurations it has given to the past, in the same way as they question the pretensions of our literary forms.

In the moments before the final blackout George, Dotty and Archie all have their final say. Dotty bids farewell to the spooney Juney Moon and George restates his claim to *know* 'that life is better than death, that love is better than hate, and that the light shining through the east window of their bloody gymnasium is more beautiful than a rotting corpse!' (p. 87). Archie, however, balances their anguish with his own elegantly phrased insouciance. 'Do not despair – ' he counsels, echoing St Augustine, 'many are happy much of the time; more eat than starve, more are healthy than sick, more curable than dying; not so many dying as dead; and one of the thieves was saved.' 'No laughter is sad' he insists, 'and many tears are joyful. At the graveside,' he ends, in idiosyncratic tribute to Beckett, 'the undertaker doffs his top hat and impregnates the prettiest mourner. Wham, bam, thank you Sam' (p. 87). This passage works in a number of ways. First, it expresses the moral detachment which makes Archie such a likely suspect for McFee's murder. Like Malquist's aesthetic of Style, the moral detachment to which Archie hopes to give philosophical respectability is not a solution to life's problems, but he claims it as a workable alternative. The fastidious accuracy of the language acts as a perfect cancellation of George's preceding tirade, which culminates in an addled roll-call of the witnesses he intends to call in support of his argument: 'Zeno Evil, St. Thomas Augustine, Jesus Moore and my late friend Herr Thumper who was as innocent as a rainbow . . .' (p. 87). In this respect, then, *Jumpers* evolves a complexity far beyond *Another Moon Called Earth*. The opposition between Penelope's emotionalism and the icy logic of Bone reappears in the conflict between George's dedication to logical philosophical enquiry and Dotty's hysterical and intuitive reaction to the ignominious struggle at the foot of the spacecraft, and is supplemented by George's impassioned rejection of Archie's smooth rationality. In effect, the speech prevents us siding wholly with George: our emotional identification with his argument is tempered by Archie's intellectual riposte. George is not allowed the unqualified status of a hero and these remarks of Archie's (though they can be seen, from one angle, as an indictment of his position) prevent solution being clapped on problem like a snuffer on a candle.

As a tribute to Beckett Archie's parting shot repeats the insights developed in *Scene:* Beckett's world is seen as having the same structure as the sentence from Augustine in which each half cancels the other. Indeed, by cancelling George so effectively, the speech performs a function in exact accordance with the principle it is asserting. Although *Jumpers* does not endorse Archie's detached rationality any more than it champions George's struggle to justify his faith on logical grounds, it does employ as a *principle of composition* that cancellation of opposites which allows Archie to retreat from their potentially painful and confusing conflict. Stoppard has said of *Jumpers* that he tends to write plays which consist of two people disputing something. 'And it's an endless debate. I don't expect one voice suddenly to produce a final statement. It's a continuing process which results in plays as far as I'm concerned.' He admits that Dotty makes two or three fairly clear observations which he considers to be 'reasonable statements, but if there were nothing to be said against them I wouldn't have written the play.'[22] Contradiction is at the very root of Stoppard's theatre; in *Jumpers* he demonstrates this principle in both the thematic content and the formal structure of the play (genre contradicting genre). In other words, (to shift our angle to the work) the play is 'about' its own form.

The fact that in *Jumpers* form is thus 'elevated' to the status of content seems to have escaped the play's detractors, who complain that it is all form and *no* content. This was evidently the case with a number of the reviewers called upon to appraise the original 1972 London production. Frank Marcus, for instance, felt that the ideas were not clear and that Stoppard's purpose was obscured: 'The effect is that of a brilliant fireworks display, which leaves little trace when the colour, sound and smoke have faded into the night.' The same point was made by John Barber who found the 'Surrealist central theme' less engrossing than the jokes and the cascades of words sent 'soaring like tailed comets'. In effect, Barber is suggesting that there is less in *Jumpers* than meets the eye (or ear) and that Stoppard is guilty of a flashy theatrical *legerdemain*. The play's formal complexity is, he maintains, exhibitionism and no more, though he does find space to complement the director, Peter Wood, for handling it all 'with a gusto that disguises the undoubted weakness in trumps of the hand he is playing.'[23]

It is, however, *Travesties* which, among Stoppard's plays, has been confronted most consistently with such criticism. Barber headlined it as a *Variable Literary Frolic* and his suspicion that the author was providing an entertaining if somewhat frivolous display was also voiced by Gerald Weales: 'Stoppard has been doing a soft shoe around existential chaos ever since he turned up in the English theatre, and *Travesties* is either his blackest statement to date or his assumption that the surface joke is what counts.' In the *Listener* John Elsom insisted that Stoppard merely used the 'theme of irrelevance' as a pad 'to launch a variety of literary pastiches'. Ken Tynan added his voice to the chorus of disapproval by suggesting that Stoppard provide more matter with less art: 'Cake, as Marie Antoinette discovered too late, is no substitute for bread.' Indeed, such references to food (and drink) are the staple diet of reviewers who find that Stoppard's play pleases the palate while failing to nourish. Frank Marcus thought *Travesties* a 'multi-layered confection' and a 'champagne cocktail', while Michael Coveney pronounced it 'a brilliant confection' but could not bring himself to describe it as a good play.[24]

Such notices, unconsciously no doubt, restate a formulation of Shaw's. Shaw claims that great artists identify their purpose with the 'purpose of the universe'. When, however, these great artists 'have travailed and brought forth and at last forced the public to associate keen pleasure and deep interest with their methods and morals, a crowd of smaller men – art confectioners, we may call them – hasten to make pretty entertainments out of scraps and crumbs from the masterpieces.'[25] The implicit accusation that Stoppard is an art confectioner does less than justice to the complexity or the effectiveness of *Travesties* – as an examination of the play (and, in particular, its relationship with *The Importance of Being Earnest*) will show.

II

David Rod has argued, in *Modern Drama*, that critics of *Travesties* have paid insufficient attention to the views on art and politics of Henry Carr, the minor consular official who regales us with his version of life as it most certainly was not in Zürich during the Great War. Carr, Rod insists, rejects the various idealisms of Tristan Tzara, James Joyce and Lenin to present an independent position of his own, founded upon a practical consideration of what art has been and what it has accomplished; Carr contributes tellingly to the debate as Stoppard creates a balance 'among the four opposing aesthetic viewpoints presented in the play, a balance that does not tip in Carr's favor even though his memory controls most of the events of the play.'[26] Rod is right to suggest that Stoppard does not allow any one of his antagonists to win the debate, but his remarks are rather beside the point. As important as *what* is said is *how* it is said; Rod's notion of a 'balance' among the four opposing viewpoints does not locate the real centre of Stoppard's dramatic strategies, which is the *form* of the play itself. It is the paramount achievement of *Travesties* that it addresses itself to the debate about the nature of art not by means of a spokesman (whether Carr or anyone else) but by its own method of procedure.

Many critics have been keen to lobby for James Joyce, to identify his as the voice of Stoppard in the great debate on art and politics.[27] Significantly, though, the play first suggested itself to Stoppard as a debate between Tzara and Lenin based on the fact that although they were in Zürich at the same time they never met: 'This seemed a rather interesting fact of history to keep in one's mind. I never quite forgot it and never quite did anything with it, and then I started working on *Travesties*.' As he did so he became 'dimly aware of James Joyce's part in all this'.[28] Lenin, of course, calls for a literature that conforms. 'Today,' he bellows at us, alone on the stage, 'literature must become party literature! Down with non-partisan literature! Down with literary supermen.'[29] His art which must not question but simply *obey* is directly opposed to the self-conscious delinquency urged by Tzara. The artist, Tzara claims, was the priest-guardian of the magic which first conjured the intelligence from the appetites, putting humanity on the first rung of the ladder to consecutive thought. His own anti-art is a protest against the abject prostitution of this exalted heritage. 'Art created patrons and was corrupted,' he raves: 'It began to celebrate the ambitions and acquisitions of the paymaster. The artist has negated himself: paint – *eat* – sculpt – grind – write – *shit*' (p. 47). Joyce's deferred entry into the scheme of things does not, of course, necessarily preclude Stoppard's turning to him as a spokesman, as an alternative to the mutual antagonism of Tzara and Lenin. What does preclude it is not just Joyce's inescapably parodic treatment but the nature of the play itself. The opposition between Tzara and Lenin restates, to some extent, that between the conformist realism of Donner and the *avant-garde*, delinquent gestures of Beauchamp; Stoppard, indeed, adapts many of the speeches from *Artist Descending a Staircase* to construct the debate in *Travesties*. Conformism and delinquency are, as we have seen, the two poles between which Stoppard's best drama in general, and *Travesties* in particular, chooses to function; in investigating that polarity Stoppard needs no spokesman, the play stands up and speaks for itself.

Travesties is unabashed in declaring the intricacy of its own design, in calling attention to its form, and the play's flamboyant cleverness has, we have noted, distressed some of its critics. Tynan's call for more matter with less art is compounded by his insistence that there is something both sterile and arbitrary at the heart of Stoppard's enterprise; he describes the imposition of Wilde's baroque plot upon the play's own burlesque version of wartime Zürich as 'crossbreeding the bizarre with the bogus'.[30] To dismiss the design of *Travesties* in such a fashion, as arbitary if brilliant, is, quite simply, wrong. Stoppard does not simply reuse the plot of *The Importance of Being Earnest*: *Travesties* is evidence of a *critical engagement* with Wilde's play. The manner of that engagement is its own statement about what art can and cannot do.

Acknowledging that, sixty years before, the confession would have won him a reputation, the young Stoppard had declared himself in the pages of the *Bristol Evening World* 'a confirmed addict and admirer (literary)' of Wilde. Noting that both Robert Morley and Peter Finch were answering the call of the Wilde in making films about his life, Stoppard claimed that 'if there is anything better than a Wilde film then it is two Wilde films'. He admitted that they should cover the subject for good 'although I suppose there is still room for a Hollywood version with Wilde (Gregory Peck) being found not guilty and going off to marry Sarah Bernhardt (Marilyn Monroe).'[31] In *Travesties* Stoppard's addiction to and admiration for Wilde are turned to good account and issue in a critical engagement with his dramatic masterpiece which is both interpretive and transformational.

Stoppard exploits *The Importance of Being Earnest*, the host-play, by pinpointing a recurrent element and elevating it to a position of ostentatious prominence. An explicit burden of literary comment runs through Wilde's original, from Jack's dismissal of modern culture as not 'the sort of thing one should talk of in private',[32] and his withering condemnation of the 'corrupt French Drama', (pp. 353–4) to Algy's claim that if life were either pure or simple modern literature would be 'a complete impossibility', (p. 352) and Gwendolen's utter certainty about the kind of play she is appearing in: 'This suspense is terrible,' she announces. 'I hope it will last' (p. 400). In *Travesties*, of course, this becomes a full-blown debate about art and the artist. Fittingly, the first-class ticket to Worthing and the cigarette case which set in motion Wilde's plot are replaced by Stoppard with a library ticket divulging Tzara's Bunburying between the Library and the Meierei Bar; if we are in any danger of accepting *The Importance of Being Earnest* as simply a social comedy of manners, the hyper-literary self-consciousness of *Travesties* ensures that we take a second look. It is interesting to note that in the closing moments of his play Stoppard cannot resist a brilliant reversal of Miss Prism's confusion of art and life when she loses baby Jack, pushing around in a pram the manuscript of her three-volume novel. Carr here parodies Lady Bracknell's half of the dialogue, thus usurping the role which up to this point had been taken by James Augusta Joyce. The remarks applied in Wilde's play to Miss Prism are here made with reference not to a person but to a manuscript of Joyce's 'Oxen of the Sun':

CARR: And is it a chapter, inordinate in length and erratic in style, remotely connected with midwifery?
JOYCE: It is a chapter which by a miracle of compression, uses the gamut of English literature from Chaucer to Carlyle to describe events taking place in a lying-in hospital in Dublin.
CARR: It is obviously the same work.

(p. 97)

The exchange has, in fact, a dual function. It prevents Joyce from claiming a victory in the battle of the books, from establishing the unquestioned pre-eminence of his way of using language. It also points to the deformation, the *ostranenie*, that Stoppard has enacted upon *The Importance of Being Earnest;* making his own substitution of art for life, he replaces the personal and social vicissitudes of Wilde's protagonists with the play's revelations about the nature of our fictions.

The Importance of Being Earnest is saturated by fictions. Each of the main characters is directly associated with a document (or documents) which counters the fictions of others and attempts to impose its own configurations upon the fictional world in which they live. In the opening scene of the play the relationship between Algy and his servant Lane is defined by Lane's book in which he keeps the household accounts. This, it transpires, is a fictional account of Algy's expenditure: a cover for Lane's plundering of the Moncrieff wine-cellar. The book, the first of the fictions to appear in the play, defines precisely the nature, extent and self-consciousness of the duplicity between master and servant. Cecily, on the other hand, has two sets of fictions: the love-letters and her diary, both of which give a completely fictional account of her relationship with the equally fictional Ernest. For Cecily, life, primarily, is of use according to the degree to which it can be turned into fiction. 'You see,' she tells Algy of her diary, 'it is simply a very young girl's record of her own thoughts and impressions and consequently meant for publication. When it appears in volume form I hope you will order a copy' (p. 377). Indeed, the conflict between Cecily and Gwendolen is bolstered by their mutual appeal to documentary evidence for verification of their respective engagements to the fictional Ernest. The announcement of her engagement will, Cecily insists, be made in 'Our little county newspaper', while Gwendolen notes, calmly, that the news of hers will 'appear in the *Morning Post* on Saturday at the latest' (p. 383). Gwendolen fights fire with fire; she matches newspaper with newspaper and the fictions of Cecily's diary are countered with those of her own. 'He asked me to be his wife yesterday afternoon at 5.30,' she maintains, 'If you would care to verify the incident, pray do so. (*Produces diary of her own.*) I never travel without my diary. One should always have something sensational to read in the train' (p. 383). In her case, no less than in Cecily's, all aspects of experience are subjected to the fictionalising mind and the contortions of fictionalising form. History itself can be contained within the contours of the 'bodice-bursting' historical melodrama. Of Jack she remarks, 'Disloyalty would be as impossible to him as deception. But even men of the noblest possible moral character are extremely susceptible to the influence of the physical charms of others. Modern, no less than Ancient History, supplies us with many most painful examples of what I refer to. If it were not so, indeed, History would be quite unreadable' (p. 382).

Gwendolen's mother, Lady Bracknell, is, of course, quite inseparable from her list of eligible young men – a document which threatens to seal Jack's fate – and Jack himself has recourse to the Army Lists to prove his assumed identity. In the original four-act version of the play this obsession with documents reaches a more explicit climax in the final scene when all the characters are handed a volume by Jack in order to track down his father's name in the army records. The Lists prove not to be what was expected of them: the meticulous researchers find themselves leafing through handsomely bound catalogues and railway timetables. These can be added to the 'certificates of Miss Cardew's birth, baptism, whooping-cough, registration, vaccination, confirmation, and the measles; both the German and the English variety' (p. 394) which Jack cites in order to prove Cecily's identity in the face of Lady Bracknell's assertion that she has known 'strange errors' (p. 393) in the Court Guides. The documents of private fiction are complemented by those of officialdom and neither proves more reliable than the other, the official publications making the fallacious and confusing claim that Jack is indeed earnest.

It is, though, Dr Chasuble's unpublished sermons which provide the most explicit comment in *The Importance of Being Earnest* on the duplicity of literary production. Chasuble calmly explains that he is ready for any eventuality. 'My sermon on the meaning of the manna in the wilderness can be adapted to almost any occasion,' he assures Jack, who has just announced the sudden demise of young Ernest, 'joyful, or, as in the present case, distressing. I have preached it at harvest celebrations, christenings, confirmations, on days of humiliation and festal days. The last time I delivered it was in the Cathedral, as a charity sermon on behalf of the Society for the Prevention of Discontent among the Upper Orders' (p. 372). Chasuble's sermons are all form, content is obliterated; far from revealing the truth, these fictions enact whatever distortions are deemed suitable. Yet it is Miss Prism who gives the most dramatic form to that substitution of art for life, of form over content, which is so vital to her social superiors. By putting the three-volume novel in the bassinette and the baby in the handbag she confuses document with person, a confusion propounded by Cecily and Gwendolen as they sensationalise their lives by means of their diaries.[33] To write is to distort. Hidden away in the closing scenes of the play is the voice of Wilde as Formalist, asserting art as lie, revelling in the impossibility of direct description:

LADY BRACKNELL: Is this Miss Prism a female of repellent aspect, remotely connected with education?
DR CHASUBLE: She is the most cultivated of ladies, and the very picture of respectability.
LADY BRACKNELL: It is obviously the same person.

(p. 398)

Miss Prism is both and neither; she exists only in terms of the lying descriptions made of her, prismatically, by others. The exchange is as vital to our pinpointing of the central strategies of *The Importance of Being Earnest* as is the parallel passage in *Travesties* to our understanding of Stoppard's tactics. This is Wilde as artist as critic, playing with the strident anti-naturalism of his *Intentions*.

'Memory, my dear Cecily,' opines Miss Prism, 'is the diary that we all carry about with us.' 'Yes,' comes the reply, 'but it usually chronicles the things that have never happened, and couldn't possibly have happened' (p. 367). This exchange, of course, reiterates the play's concern with the untrustworthiness of all writing: the diary is assimilated to the sensationalising activities of the imagination. The remark would also seem to give Stoppard his cue in *Travesties*. The play is under the erratic control of Old Carr's memory, telling of things that did not happen, and couldn't possibly have happened, in pacific Switzerland during the Great War.[34] His memory lies in the way that all fiction lies, and his rewriting of history is, at a basic level, a dismissive parody of that most 'truth-telling' of all fictional forms, the Lukácsian historical novel. Lukács identifies as a fundamental technique of the historical novelist the use of a hero from the middle rank whose adventures shed light on the fabric of society as he encounters both high and low, the representatives of the people and the world-historical personalities.[35] Carr is such a hero, his adventures bringing him into contact with the great champions of art and anti-art and the world-historical personality of Lenin. In *Travesties*, however, the hero places himself very much centre-stage: history, and the society in which he has lived, are displayed solely in order to show the part he has, or has not, played in them. Carr, in the act of reminiscence, is attempting to define his own relevance. Just as Rosencrantz and his partner attempt to grasp their significance in the story of Hamlet, so Carr attempts to define his in relation to Lenin's flight from Switzerland and the events which followed. In fact, Old Cecily reminds him of the fictional nature of the dilemma he has posed himself; he had never really been the Consul and, by the time he came to play Algy, Lenin had long gone. The play's view of history is, in other words, far from objective in the Lukácsian sense but is, according to Peter Wood (who directed the first production), 'seen prismatically through the view of Henry Carr. At one point Tom was thinking of calling it "Prism" . . .'.[36] The echo of *The Importance of Being Earnest* is quite unmistakable. Memory is the diary that Carr carries with him; his chronicle imposes a whole gallery of stereotyped images and figures upon his fictional experience, and memory is seen to function in the same duplicitous way as the fictionalising imagination.

Travesties is replete with stereotypes. We have James Joyce as a comic stage-Irishman, speaking in limericks and looking for a loan, Tristan Tzara as a Rumanian nonsense complete with monocle and fractured English. At one point in the second act the stage is dominated by a huge slide of Lenin, captured on celluloid in an attitude of iron-willed resolution: '*a justly famous image*' (p. 84). Parenthetically, but significantly, Stoppard adds '*This is the photo, incidentally, which Stalin had retouched so as to expunge Kamenev and Trotsky who feature prominently in the original*' (p. 85). History has frozen into familiar form, and that form is a lie. The public lie of the historical stereotype is complemented by Carr's private lies. He refashions himself and his rivals in the same way as the characters in *The Importance of Being Earnest* use the established literary types of the wicked brother, the officious guardian, the gorgon-aunt and so on, to give shape and significance to their lives. To stereotype people is to control them, and this is precisely what Carr is attempting to do, to slot himself into a history which, apparently, has largely passed him by.

When recasting the events he purports to recall in the overall shape of *The Importance of Being Earnest* Carr takes the role of Algy, transmuting the egoism of the Dandy, living solely for pleasure, into that of the peripheral figure who will no longer be ignored. His sense that identity can only truly be appraised through action (defining who he *is* by what he has *done*, what significance he has attained) allows Carr to assign Lenin a supporting role in his own personal drama. 'I might have stopped the whole Bolshevik thing in its tracks,' he tells Old Cecily, 'but, here's the point. *I was uncertain*' (p. 81). 'And don't forget,' he continues, plaintively, *'he wasn't Lenin then! I mean who was he?* as it were' (p. 81). The shifting of perspective which comes with historical insight makes direct description a plain impossibility: there is no 'natural' way of describing the Lenin who knew the rented obscurity of 14 Spiegelgasse. Such a consciousness of the relativity of historical evaluation sanctions Carr's own History as Egoism and his exuberant espousal of an enormously variegated range of possible ways of describing and proving what did, and did not, happen.

The fundamental lesson of *The Importance of Being Earnest* is that all writing is a lie we cannot do without. In the debate with which *Travesties* plays, documents are used as offensive weapons: memoirs (Gorki's, Fritz Platten's), letters (Lenin's to Karpinsky, his memos to Lunacharsky and Gorki), diary extracts (Hugo Ball's), legal documents (court records of the Bezirksgericht Zuerich) and public speeches (Lenin's) are referred to, cited or quoted by the various antagonists in order to make their version of history prevail. *Travesties*, however, demonstrates a complete breakdown in the hierarchy of evidence: no single document or form of written proof (particularly newspapers: the *Neue Zuricher Zeitung* and the *Zuricher Post* contradict each other in their partisan reports on the state of the war as completely as the *Morning Post* and its rival in their announcement of Ernest's engagements) or argument is allowed to silence the others. Similarly, and crucially, the play refuses to admit that any single *style* of writing enjoys a uniquely privileged relationship with what it purports to transcribe: the play is an argument between styles to match its argument between documents. The opening scene shows Stoppard's basic tactic at work: in the library Lenin's Russian is set alongside Tzara's verbal hat-trick, a quotation from Lenin's papers, snippets of *Ulysses* and Cecily's 'Ssssssh!' which is, ironically, the only utterance we fully understand. The scene prepares us for the sheer range of parody and interpolation that the play will have at its command. Joyce contributes limericks, a rendition of *Mr Dooley* and an interrogation of Tzara in the constabular style of the 'Ithaca' section of *Ulysses*. Carr contributes massacred dialogue from *The Importance of Being Earnest* and his own idiosyncratic prose steeped in travel-brochure clichés. Cecily lectures us on the history of Leninism and joins Gwendolen in a parody of a Gallagher and Sheen routine. Tzara brings us English in a variety of forms including comic pidgin and mangled Shakespearean verse. Carr summons the historical giants to the stage, lets them have their say, and then dismisses them. The play invokes style after style, exploits each to the point of exhaustion, and moves on.

Stoppard's sensitivity, then, to Wilde's metafictional preoccupations (the involution of his critical concerns with his dramatic practice) sanctions his own use of extensive parody and stereotypes and his focus on the role of duplicitous fictions in the making of our meanings, the encoding of our world. Interpretation and transformation of Wilde's play go hand in hand; at its most playful *Travesties* reduces *The Importance of Being Earnest* to a series of costume-changes. As summarised by Joyce to the sartorially fastidious Carr the play *is* nothing but looks everything. 'The curtain rises,' explains Joyce, 'A flat in Mayfair. Teatime. You enter in a bottle-green velvet smoking jacket with black frogging – hose white, cravat perfect, boots elastic-sided, trousers,' he adds, ominously, 'of your own choice . . . Act Two. A rose garden. After lunch. Some by-play among the small parts. You enter in a debonair garden-party outfit – beribboned boater, gaily striped blazer, parti-coloured shoes, trousers of your own choice'(p.52). This is, indeed, a triumph of form over content, and again it points to (burlesques almost) Stoppard's own way with *The Importance of Being Earnest:* he brings the form of the play into the very foreground, makes it a subject of attention. The structure of Wilde's play is that of travesty: Jack's proposal to Gwendolen is played again, and travestied, by Cecily and Algy; Lady Bracknell's interrogation of Jack in Act One reappears in a different form in her haranguing of Miss Prism. Similarly, individual scenes are themselves structured by travesty with one voice restating and confounding the other. It is precisely according to this principle that *Travesties* assembles itself.

Travesties has an argument with itself, constantly doubling-back to contradict and deny those shapes it has given to the past. Tzara, for instance, first enters as a *'Rumanian nonsense'* (p.32). This is both a parody of Jack Worthing's first entrance and itself the subject of later parody. Soon this Rumanian joke is joined by an Irish joke: Joyce spouting limericks and looking for a loan. Carr's memory hurtles spectacularly off the rails as the entire scene is played out in limericks (pp.33–6). Tzara, however, re-enters when this frenetic dialogue has exhausted itself. This time he is straight out of *The Importance of Being Earnest*, exhibiting a 'perfect English languor'.[37] Carr swaps one stereotype for another; he criticises one patently ludicrous version of history and embarks upon another that is equally untenable. The central contention of Wilde's *Intentions* is that art which pretends to reproduce mimetically is a lie and that the only honest alternative is to turn this vice into a virtue. Carr's chronicle is almost a parody of the literature Wilde intends, criticising one set of lies by means of another.

Travesty and contradiction are evident even at the fundamental level of language. The text of *Travesties* is woven together by repetition: phrases, turns of expression recur in travestied, often contradictory, form. In the replaying of the scene in which Carr and Tzara discuss politics and art the reversal of initiative is expressed through a repeated verbal pattern. First, Tzara's heated dismissal of the traditional sophistries for waging wars of expansion and self-interest brings forth Carr's pained protest that 'You are insulting my comrades-in-arms, many of whom died on the field of honour' (p.39). In the second version, Carr counters Tzara's belief in the importance of art by describing it as, in essence, simply a beautifier of existence and denying that it can lay claim to any serious political efficacy. Tzara's cold rebuff is a pointed travesty of what has gone before: 'You are insulting me and my comrades in the Dada Exhibition' (p.46). Repetition is employed specifically for the purpose of contradiction. At times, however, repetition evolves towards a higher complexity. This is the case when Carr infiltrates the library and attempts to woo Cecily, Lenin's devotee. The scene parodies, of course, that in which Algy attempts to woo Cecily, while posing as Ernest. Yet this parody is itself reflected in another as it develops into a travesty of the earlier discussion between Carr and Tzara. Once more we are given successive versions of the same scene and verbal motifs are repeated and travestied. In high dudgeon Cecily rejects Carr's critique of Marxist theory: 'you are insulting me and my comrades – ' (p. 76). Once again, Stoppard's art is a hinged mirror, in which the leaves reflect nothing but each other.

The self-inspection and self-contradiction in the play's structure is reflected not just in repeated verbal motifs, but also in the very prose itself. It is in Carr's opening monologue that Stoppard's dramatic prose denies and cancels itself most effectively. There is, indeed, an irony here. 'If there is any point in using language at all,' he insists to Tzara, 'it is that a word is taken to stand for a particular fact or idea and not for other facts or ideas' (p. 38). This is a precept Carr can hardly be said to put into practice: his own speeches pay no such attention to the conventional division of sense and nonsense. Each of his descriptions is immediately cancelled as the prose advances in a halting parody of the deferential friend of the famous who no sooner attributes a quality to a great man than he feels impelled to deny that it is in any way carried to excess. Joyce exhibits 'a monkish unconcern for worldly and bodily comforts, without at the same time shutting himself off from the richness of human society, whose temptations, on the other hand, he met with an ascetic disregard tempered only by sudden and catastrophic aberrations,' (p. 23). Carr's description of life in Zürich is couched in a prose which takes no account of the external state of affairs it is supposed to transcribe. Ever watchful, it advances by denying and criticising itself. ''Twas in the bustling metropolis of swiftly gliding trams and greystone banking houses,' he begins, establishing a closed field of linguistic possibilities within which he then proceeds to play, 'of cosmopolitan restaurants on the great stone banks of the swiftly-gliding snot-green (mucus mutandis) Limmat River, of jewelled escapements and refugees of all kind, e.g. Lenin,' (p. 23). This is prose as self-evident sham: the trams are mentioned purely to pun on *bus*tling, the great stone banks present a critical reworking of greystone banking houses, the river is snot-green by virtue of the excruciating Latin pun it facilitates. The 'naturalness' of the description is also undercut by the river's murky literary parentage. Its progenitors are Joyce's 'grey sweet mother' the 'snotgreen sea'[38] and Kipling's 'great grey-green greasy Limpopo River'.[39] A little later Carr works a further variation on his material: 'Meet by the sadly-sliding chagrinned Limmat River,' he counsels, 'strike west and immediately we find ourselves soaking wet, strike east and immediately we find ourselves in the Old Town, having left behind the banking bouncing metropolis of trampolines and chronometry of all kinds for here time has stopped' (p. 24).

Hersh Zeifman suggests, in attempting to locate Stoppard's allegiances, that the plethora of puns in the play is its most effective stratagem nudging us towards Joyce's point of view.[40] Yet the puns are less a veiled acknowledgement of literary influence than a function of the play's structure. The design of *Travesties* is the design of denial; self-inspection and self-contradiction are combined in self-criticism as the play continually examines its own conventions and terms of existence. The puns deny the claims of the prose to describe the world, proclaiming its processes as fictionalisation; they contradict both the primary, transitional sense attempted and the claims of Carr that, for language to work, a word must be taken to stand for a particular fact or idea and not for other facts or ideas. When seen in this way the puns do indeed help to locate Stoppard's allegiances. The presiding genius of *Travesties* is not Joyce, but Oscar Wilde: the Wilde who, in his criticism and his drama, championed a literature which, by contradicting its own claims to tell the truth, could tell a truth of sorts.

'All poetry,' says Tzara, offering Gwendolen a scissored sonnet in his hat, 'is a reshuffling of a pack of picture cards, and all poets are cheats' (p. 53). 'Cleverness,' he has told Carr earlier, 'has been exploded, along with so much else, by the war' (p. 37). By offering Gwendolen Shakespeare's eighteenth sonnet drawn at random and piecemeal from a hat he hopes to deny that rational premeditation of the creative act which has led to its prostitution. His rewriting of the artist's signature in the hand of chance is also a protest against the indigence of traditional art, the tired tricks it works with an all-too familiar routine. In a sense, Old Carr's memory works in precisely the same way: reshuffling the picture-cards of the past, cheating history with the dog-eared trump-card of *The Importance of Being Earnest*. In an important sense, however, his approach differs from that of the anti-artist and the traditional artist; the form of the play is a contradiction, a denial, of the traditionalism of the views Carr expresses. Unlike Tzara he does not abandon design to chance, but unlike the traditionalist he makes no attempt to disguise the trick he is playing. Old Carr does not just pull history from a hat, nor does he rest easy with the form it has been allowed to assume. He tells it in his own lying, designing way.

In fact, and typically, Stoppard's play refuses the stark choice presented by conformism and delinquency, by art and anti-art, by the twin peaks of the pendulum swing. This refusal is an act of criticism: by isolating and using techniques employed by both alternatives (creating design, for instance, which denies design) *Travesties* frees itself from each. Stoppard seizes the pendulum and speeds it to the beat of his will. *Travesties* is an acute refinement of Stoppard's Theatre of Criticism; at all levels (from its engagement with *The Importance of Being Earnest*, to its anthologising of divergent styles and its marshalling of mutually exclusive arguments) we can see that disciplined observation of, and conformity to, established ways of seeing, thinking and saying coupled with the sudden and pointed departure therefrom which is the province of the critical work.

In *The Importance of Being Earnest* 'playing' is the attainment of freedom. The two pairs of young lovers undergo a process of self-creation, becoming the fabrications of their own fictionalising imaginations. 'The only thing that one really knows about human nature,' claims Wilde, 'is that it changes. Change is the one quality we can predicate of it' (p. 283). The lovers in this quintessential comedy of disguise and mistaken identity make a virtue of the changeability that Wilde proclaims; they learn the truth of masks, that personality can be constructed by a critical refusal to leave well alone. It is this conscious espousal of duplicity which fascinates Wilde. The actor and the Bunburyist are united in their 'playing' and become types of the artist who asserts his dissatisfaction with a narrowly-conceived notion of truth-telling by indulging in the brazen and palpable lie. Stoppard's Henry Carr attempts to reconstruct his history and personality in the same way as Wilde's young lovers; this is a gesture towards self-definition and freedom, the manner of this gesture (his continual recourse to literary and historical stereotypes) is a recognition of restraint. In effect, Carr 'plays with' the past in the same way as Stoppard 'plays with' literary procedure, displaying it to deny it, criticising it in the act of freeing himself from it. 'Playfulness' in both *Travesties* and *The Importance of Being Earnest* is not just a spirit of fun, it is the act of criticism itself.

In *The Soul of Man Under Socialism* Wilde extends his anti-naturalism from the literary to the political sphere, announcing his contempt for all political systems which interfere with the fundamental human right, and need, to change; his literary concerns receive a consistent political articulation in his assertion of the need to reject and replace prevailing social, political and institutional forms. Annoyed by Carr's description of Wilde as indifferent to politics, Ken Tynan rightly commends *The Soul of Man Under*

Socialism to anyone who believes this and claims that the hard polemical purpose of *Travesties* is to argue that art must be independent of politics.[41] Yet, if we acknowledge the way in which the form of the play contradicts the traditionalism of Carr's views, we can see that Tynan is wrong and that *Travesties*, in doing so, makes a far more positive assertion, and one of which Wilde would have approved: that art can embody a freedom that is inseparable from criticism. The 'play' of *Travesties*, the brilliance and the point of its design, is a refusal and a criticism of the available alternatives of freedom and delinquency; the play needs no spokesman to free itself from the claims of a Lenin or a Tzara alike. In the true spirit of Oscar Wilde, and by means of a critical engagement with his masterpiece, Stoppard has produced a play which has earned its liberty and taken none.

Part II

Part II

5

The Dissenters

I

Creation, for Stoppard, is dissent. His drama, at its best, is not simply a gesture of refusal: it earns its liberty, as we have seen, by means of a critical engagement with the demands of conformity. Dissent is, for the artist, both invigorating and necessary; for Stoppard's spiritual loners (that long succession of his characters who refuse the common ground), it is necessarily painful and disabling. In his more recent work the loner as tame believer, as bemused mystic consigned and resigned to the periphery, becomes the loner as political dissident. There is nothing arbitrary about this explicit appearance of politics in Stoppard's work; it bears witness to his continued engagement with the problem of criticism. However, an examination of the ways in which the early dissenters develop into the dissidents will prepare the way for our understanding of how Stoppard betrays himself into a contradiction of his own aesthetics of engagement.

We have already seen how in *Enter a Free Man* George Riley, the first of Stoppard's dissenters, fails to arrive at a set of authentic values of his own; his grandly-conceived revolt simply amounts to a retreat into the fantasy of his inventions. Riley's immediate successors (Gladys, John Brown and Albert) have none of Riley's self-conscious exuberance, but they do share his failure: a failure determined by the very nature of their dissent. Like Dotty, in *Jumpers*, they have seen that society's truths have edges and this terrible knowledge has, to varying degrees, unhinged them all. In essence, they display a common reaction to a world that has been nudged into grotesque outline. Their spiritual revolt becomes a form of spiritual retreat.

In *If You're Glad, I'll be Frank* the common ground that Gladys refuses is the prevailing, collective experience of time. The scale of human life has been reduced: far above the tiny world of the Post

Office and her bus-driver husband's enslavement to his timetable,
Gladys feels only spiritual dislocation, a sense of vertigo:

> When you look down from
>   a great height
> you become dizzy. Such
>   depth, such distance,
> such disappearing tininess so
>   far away,
> rushing away,
> reducing the life-size to
>   nothing –
> it upsets the scale you live by[1]

The eyes go first, she tells us, followed by the head and if you can't
look away you feel sick. 'And that's my view of time – ' (p. 45).

What is quite clear is that Gladys's dissent from the common
notion of time is a form of retreat. She remembers her first meeting
with Frank (who 'had all the time in the world for me, such as it
was' (p. 53)) and in so doing expresses her pained new awareness
of time:

> There was time to laugh then
> but while I laughed a bumblebee
> fluttered its wings a million times
>   (p. 52)

Gladys has turned her back on the frenetic activity of her fellows
who think that time is something they invented 'for their own
convenience' (p. 44). She insists that time is impartial, disinterested
and godlike and her new sense of scale spreads our truths thinner
and thinner until they disappear into nullity:

> I'd be only in
>   the middle of it,
>   with an inkling of infinity,
>   the only one who has seen both
>   ends,
>   rushing away from the middle
>   (p. 48)

Like Malquist, she knows time as a vast immutability which reduces the human scale: the anxieties and ambitions of everyday life become as insect movements in the grass. She turns from them, as from the sufferings of her husband, in quiet contempt. We learn that she had hoped, initially, for a refuge in a nunnery, but had been refused because of her religious doubts. The play ends with Frank's failure to free her from her self-inflicted prison, and with her continuing unspoken dissent from her own public voice, the Speaking Clock.

John Brown, the central character of *A Separate Peace* (broadcast as a television play in 1966, the same year as *If You're Glad, I'll be Frank* was performed on the radio) provides a further, and perhaps fuller, anatomy of dissent as retreat. Brown, who books out of life and into the Beechwood Nursing Home, comes from out of nowhere in search of a sort of monastery for agnostics and thinks that he has found such a sanctuary in the private hospital. Safely ensconced in his private ward (despite the puzzled attempts of the hospital authorities to establish his identity and explain the holdalls of money with which he pays his bills) Brown begins to paint a huge mural: 'Hospital routine in a pastoral setting. That's a kind of perfection, really.'[2] The Doctor feels that Brown is disturbingly self-sufficient and his patient admits that it is the self-sufficient separateness of the hospital which impresses him: 'The matron does her round, not affected by anything outside. You need never know anything, it doesn't touch you.' However, at the very moment he proclaims most enthusiastically the virtues of the Beechwood Nursing Home, Brown, quite consciously, contradicts himself:

MAGGIE: That's not true, Brownie.
BROWN: I know it's not.
MAGGIE: Then you shouldn't try and make it true.
BROWN: I know I shouldn't.

(p. 179)

The world, it transpires, is still too much with John Brown.

The play reveals that this self-sufficiency is fraudulent. Brown's flight from 'Fire, flood and misery of all kinds,' (p. 178) is established as firmly egocentric. We learn that he has once before discovered such a sanctuary from a world flying apart – as a Prisoner of War: 'Up to then it was all terrible. Chaos – all the pins must have fallen off the map, dive bombers and bullets. Oh dear, yes. The camp was like breathing out for the first time in months. I couldn't believe it.

It was like winning, being captured' (p. 180). The war continues, but Brown, scorning the attempts of his fellow prisoners to escape, has contracted his own separate peace 'in a box of earth and wire and sky' (p. 181). The point is clear: Brown's dream of self-sufficient withdrawal is mediated indeed – his 'white calm' (p. 174) in the hospital is sustained only by others prepared to minister to his needs and the comforts of imprisonment are built from the sufferings of others. Brown cannot be set loose from the world and his persistence in attempting to make his fantasy come true is a refined form of self-indulgence.

In returning to the hospital Brown admits that he is trying to recover the consolations of childhood – that 'safe area' and ordered world lauded by both Mr Moon and Guildenstern. His dissent is not just withdrawal, it is also regression; Brown's dissatisfaction with a world out of joint is displaced by his flagrant abnegation of responsibility. In effect, Brown's confession to Maggie cancels his own position in two ways. His growing affection for the nurse belies his claims to self-sufficiency and, by prompting him to reveal that he had stayed in the hospital as a child, it leads to the discovery of his identity. 'You couldn't leave well alone, could you?' snaps Brown when the Doctor confronts him with his knowledge of the facts. 'It's not enough, Mr Brown,' he insists, 'You've got to . . . *connect* . . .' (p. 183). Brown, of course, has made contact – with Maggie – and it is his relationship with her which both destroys his temporary sanctuary and allows him to continue his retreat, for it is Maggie who allows his nocturnal escape from the anxious ministrations of his family. 'If I'd been *sick*,' he notes ruefully, 'I would have been all right' (p. 183).

Albert's Bridge centres on another spiritual loner who, in attempting to set himself loose from the world, turns resolutely from his family: in this case, his wife and child. Albert believes that in the bridge to which he dedicates his life to painting he has discovered the anchored viewpoint, the mental *terra firma*, from which the contours of experience will assume recognisable and manageable shape. From his new perspective, high above the town, Albert sees terrestrial confusion assemble itself into logical order. Everything is placed, including his own past life as a philosophy student: 'I saw more up there in three weeks than those dots did in three years. I saw the context. It reduced philosophy and everything else. I got a perspective.'[3] The bridge represents formal poise denying chaos: an iron-girdered triumph of Malquist's Aesthetic of Style. To Albert it is 'separate – complete – removed, defined by principles of engineering which make it stop at a certain point, which compels a certain shape, certain joints – the whole thing utterly fixed by the rules that make it stay up' (p. 16). 'A man,' he notes, proudly, 'can give his life to its maintenance, a very fine bargain' (p. 16). Seen from his elevated position, the urban sprawl becomes the most expensive toytown in the store: 'I tremble for it, half expecting some petulant pampered child to step over the hill and kick the whole thing to bits with her Startrite sandals' (p. 22). In other words, Albert's sense of the fragility of what had once seemed to him both cloying and immensely confused betrays him into a feeling of contempt. 'I could,' he says of the dots, bricks and beetles below, 'drown them in my spit' (p. 24). The instant disclaimer ('It doesn't represent desire. I'll let them live. I'm only trying to tell you what it's like' (p. 24)) cannot dispel the impression that Albert is the spiritual loner as prig, that his dissent is a fastidious washing of the hands.

'Monsieur Eiffel, poet and philosopher,' declares Albert, 'every eight years I'll scratch your name in the silver of Clufton Bay Bridge,' (p. 27). The invocation is pointed: Eiffel's tower does not compromise itself with function in the way that bridges do and Albert associates its pristine autonomy with the consolations of perfected aesthetic form no less than with those of philosophy. Form is to him a safe-area and a retreat, as it is to Brown, sitting inside his painting, and to Malquist, horrified by the prospect of drinking *crème de menthe* in a pale blue cravat. Indeed, Albert's retreat is no more successful than theirs. He is destroyed by the massed energy of toytown: eighteen hundred marching painters who fail to break step and thus shatter the perfection of his bridge.

If Albert's withdrawal parallels that of Malquist, then Fraser's plight can be seen as restating that of Moon. Both are convinced of apocalypse now, that, as Fraser puts it, 'the shell of human existence is filling out, expanding, and it's going to go bang – ' (p. 30). 'The outside edge,' he repeats, later, 'is filling out like a balloon, without the assurance of infinity' (p. 37).[4] Moon dismisses the notion that he is psychotic but insists that he is just wide-open to certain things, and Fraser repeats this self-diagnosis: 'I am simply open, wide open, to certain insights. I do not believe that there is anyone in control' (p. 30). Like Moon, Fraser has a recurring lack of faith in his own dissent. He tells Albert that 'down there' he is assailed by the flying splinters of a world breaking up, but once on the bridge 'I look down at it all and find that the proportions have been re-established. My confidence is restored, by perspective' (p. 37). In retreat from the enormity of social disorder, Fraser continually climbs up 'to cast myself off, without faith in angels to catch me – or desire that they should' (p. 37), only to decide that the common ground can be occupied, after all: 'Yes, from a vantage point like this, the idea of society is just about tenable' (p. 32). Albert's reply is characteristically uncompromising: 'Funked it. Well, mind how you go. Don't fall' (p. 32). For Fraser, a consummate verbalist, words are not so much a solution to his confusions as a workable alternative.

Curiously, Stoppard's adaptation from the Polish of Slawomir Mrozek's *Tango*, first performed by the Royal Shakespeare Company in 1966, which is roughly contemporaneous with *A Separate Peace* and *If You're Glad, I'll be Frank*, contains a significant deepening in his portrayal of the spiritual loner. In Arthur, the son who rebels against his parents and attendant relations, Mrozek investigates the nature of dissent – and the nature of freedom. Arthur, too, is an equivocal figure whose spiritual revolt is as painful and disabling, as frustrated and as mediated, as is that of Stoppard's own *dramatis personae*. The attraction of *Tango* to Stoppard is clear: Mrozek's treatment of the relationship between revolt and conformity and freedom and delinquency (and his willingness to implicate art in this discussion) is framed in terms that Stoppard had hammered-out for himself in the pages of *Scene*. Essentially, Arthur has a more complex understanding of the nature of freedom, an understanding which recognises the redundancy of gestures of refusal and retreat.

Tango is founded upon an inversion of the standard situation of family comedy, or the 'plot-riddled uproar of domestic crisis'. Arthur's mother is appalled by the idea of her son becoming a doctor, recalling her hopes that he would be an artist: 'While I still carried him in my womb I used to run naked through the woods, singing Bach cantatas . . . I might as well have stayed at home.'[5] Eleanor and her husband, Stomil, look back with nostalgia upon the exuberant iconoclasm of their youth. 'As far as I remember,' says Stomil, countering his wife's claim that the first time they broke with tradition was when they made love in front of her mother and father during the première of *Tannhäuser*, 'it was in the National Gallery during the Modern Art Exhibition. We got rave notices' (p. 109). This spirit of sexual and artistic revolt lives on in the pair's domestic arrangements. Stomil continues his never-ending search for new ways of artistic experiment, clad in pyjamas that proudly flaunt an unbut-

toned fly; Eleanor sleeps with the loutish Eddie, unable to compre-
hend the righteous disgust of her son. Artists, declares Arthur, are
a plague upon the earth, 'they were the first to undermine the age'
(p. 123).

Arthur recoils from the domestic disorder that surrounds him.
'This house is a bedlam of anarchy and chaos!' he screams, 'Grandfather has been dead ten years. And no one has thought of taking
away that catafalque. It's unbelievable. It's a wonder they took
Grandfather away' (p. 107). The opening moments of the play, as
Arthur rages amid the clutter of absurdist bric-à-brac on stage in an
attempt to break up his family's card-school, establish the consequences of Stomil's claim that man has toppled the old gods and
climbed up onto the pedestal. 'Down with the old forms,' announces
Stomil, 'crack convention wide open and long live the new life –
dynamic, creative, free, beyond form! – oh, yes – beyond form!' (p.
109). It is precisely this last claim that Arthur denies: he refuses to
accept that a life beyond form is either creative or free. His father
dismisses his objections as decadent, describing him as 'the first man
to have principles for fifty years' (p. 158). Stomil recalls that his
generation would have rather perished than conformed: 'To rebel!
– that was the only thing of any value.' Arthur's reply – 'What
value?' (p. 111) – crystallises his mounting despair and his conviction
that a world beyond form is a world without significance.

In essence, Arthur is the only member of his family aware of the
paradox of rebellion. If to rebel is the only thing of value, what
happens when all the chains have been broken, all the fetters
smashed, and there is nothing left to rebel against? 'With you,' he
accuses his father, 'freedom is compulsory! – immorality is a moral
obligation' (p. 111). Consequently, Arthur feels that he has been
denied any chance of asserting his individuality: 'You've been kicking
over the totems for so long that there's nothing left for me to kick
against – nothing! Abnormality is the new norm, and all I've got to
rebel against is you and your muck' (p. 113). Freedom, he feels, has
come to mean the same as delinquence: it has become a simple
gesture of refusal. His self-imposed task is to bring meaning back to
freedom – and to establish a set of values. It is, however, in his
attempt to establish these values that we witness the frustration and
the mediation of Arthur's revolt.

He tries, for instance, to give meaning and value to the (to him)
distasteful relationship between his parents and Eddie by giving it
the formal unity of art: he tries to direct his own domestic tragedy.

He tries to goad Stomil into murderous revenge, but his father will have none of it: 'Tragedy has always been the final throw of societies based on rigid ideas. So you thought you'd push me into a tragic act' (pp. 139–40). On the other hand, Arthur insists that tragedy is a great and powerful convention – and that reality would be trapped within it. Stomil remains unconvinced: 'You know what you are?' he asks, pursuing his belief that reality is stronger than any convention, 'you're just a dirty little formalist. You don't give a damn about me, or your mother. They can all drop dead so long as the form is preserved' (p. 140). Arthur, in other words, is seen by Stomil as a formalist in Susan Sontag's pejorative sense of the word: he is persisting in the employment of outworn and outmoded aesthetic formulae. Stomil insists that if he did shoot Eddie, all Arthur would get is a farce: 'Today farce is the only thing possible. A corpse is no help at all. Why not accept this? – Farce can still be fine art' (p. 141). Fine art or not, Arthur soon has a farce on his hands; when Stomil finally breaks down and seizes the revolver he storms into the bedroom to find his wife and Eddie *in flagrante delicto* – playing cards.

Although Arthur fails in his attempt to give his home life meaning as Tragedy, he is adamant that a showcase wedding to his cousin Ala will reassert the fundamental importance of form. Despite the fact that Ala seems temperamentally incapable of acting-out the time-honoured ritual of pursuit and final surrender, Arthur tries to insist on a return to conventional behaviour; he points out that a major advantage of this return to form is the possibility it creates for the unexpected. 'I didn't behave to pattern,' boasts Arthur when he resists the temptations offered by the scantily-clad Ala, 'and you were intrigued. It was exceptional and that gave it value. And so I gave meaning to our meaningless encounter – I did it' (p. 125). The wedding itself will be a shock-tactic. 'It must take them by surprise,' he insists, echoing Moon's hope that, with his bomb, he can shock people into a recognition that things have gone badly wrong, 'they must have no chance to collect themselves and organize resistance and break up what I've started. We shall strike immediately and at the heart, so fast that once the formalities have taken hold of them they won't be able to escape' (p. 133).

Unfortunately for Arthur, his attempt to conjure significance by means of the wedding is as comprehensive a farce as his earlier attempt to rewrite his life as Tragedy. Act Three opens with a tableau exhibiting the effects of Arthur's counter-revolution. Uncle Eugene,

Arthur's accomplice, has arranged the family (stock-still in clothes just out of mothballs, in a room showing no trace of its former disorder) into a group photograph, even though his camera does not work. 'Right now,' he explains to the sceptical Stomil, 'we have to concentrate on form. Content comes later' (p. 154). Stomil, for his part, is saddened by such decadence: 'Formalism won't free us from chaos. We'd do better to come to terms with the spirit of the times' (p. 155). This is precisely the realisation that dawns on the desperate Arthur. The grotesque spectacle convinces him that the old conventions will not bring back reality and he acknowledges the justice of his father's accusations: 'I'm just a pathetic formalist' (p. 165). Instead of tradition, Arthur now argues for a 'living idea' to sanction the cause of order and value – an idea that will give him form. It is his solution to the paradox of freedom – the problem of how to create enduring order through the significant act of rebellion – that displays the equivocal nature of his insistent dissent.

Arthur's living idea is Power. In it, he claims, rebellion is joined with order and contradiction is destroyed. Indeed, power *is* rebellion: 'Rebellion in the form of order, the top against the bottom, the high against the low. There can be no high without a low and no low without a high – and that's what power is all about: the opposites don't cancel each other out, but define one another' (p. 174). Power will give Arthur the form he yearns for, 'any form I fancy, not one but a thousand possibilities. I can create and demolish at will, it's all within me, here!' (p. 174). Arthur's rhetoric exposes him neatly. The ideology of power proclaims the triumph of his egoism: 'I am your redeemer, you vacant cattle. I shall embrace you all, because I have a mind independent of stomachs and digestions, I have a mind!' (p. 172). It is also a sinister echo of George Riley's comic determination to prove himself the type of the individual mind that raises itself above the common herd. Arthur admits that his 'pathetic formalism' was a retreat into the past. Yet the final twist to his spiritual revolt is itself a further withdrawal – to the consolations of the ego. Indeed, far from order, the counter-revolution simply brings further dissolution because Arthur's ascent to power entails Eddie's destructive violence. His proud boast to be able to create and demolish at will is denied almost as soon as it is made. Eddie pistol-whips him, deftly pushes his head forward and kills him with a single blow of his clenched fists. Arthur's failure is determined precisely by the nature of his revolt; he is swept away by the very violence he has himself released. In seeking a social order which will enable both creativity and freedom Arthur succeeds in establishing their very opposite and in renewing the principle of cancellation. The play ends with Eddie, in Arthur's jacket, and Eugene, with red carnation buttonhole, dancing a tango around Arthur's body to *La Camparsita*. The curtain thus comes down on the tableau as absurd as that with which the play opened. This time, however, we have witnessed the way that absurdity has been constructed from logic, the logic of Arthur's ideology of power. In *After Magritte*, of course, Stoppard went on to present us with much the same process (logic proliferating into absurdity) and the play, with its opening and closing tableaux, owes an obvious debt to the structure of *Tango*.

Martin Esslin points out that to the first audience of *Tango*, in the Warsaw of 1964, the play had seemed a bitter and sardonic comment on Stalinism and its totalitarian structure of terror.[6] Mrozek's Bohemian family reflects the confusions of life between the wars counterpointed by the ominous nostalgia of reaction; the peculiar power of *Tango* lies precisely in its exploitation of Absurdist devices within the disciplines of debate and clear, if not specific, historical context. Stoppard's *Jumpers* is a comparable achievement; if the historical context is not full-blown, the philosophical context most certainly is. George Moore certainly represents an advance on the spiritual loners who precede him. In his philosophical tussles with the prevailing orthodoxy he encounters not only the problem of criticism, but also an opponent which denies its very possibility. George, indeed, is vital to our understanding of how the Stoppardian dissenters of the early work develop into the political dissidents of the later.

II

George Moore, refusing to bend his knees in *Jumpers*, points out that the book which would have made his name was to be called *Language, Truth and God*. 'An American publisher,' he explains, 'has expressed an interest but he wants to edit it himself and change the title to *You Better Believe It*' (p. 58). He declares it his intention to set British philosophy back forty years, 'which is roughly when it went off the rails' (p. 46). The paper he hopes to deliver to the philosophical symposium is structured, accordingly, around a protracted critique of A. J. Ayer's *Language, Truth and Logic* which first transplanted the doctrines of the Vienna Circle from Teutonic to British soil when published in 1936. There is, says Jonathan Bennett in his article 'Philosophy and Mr Stoppard', no structural relationship between such academic philosophical material and the rest of the play: compared to the philosophical content of *Rosencrantz and Guildenstern are Dead*, which is 'solid, serious and functional',[7] George's academic struggles are thin and uninteresting, serving *Jumpers* in only a marginal and decorative way. As a critical judgement this is as spectacularly wide of the mark as the arrow with which George hopes to put paid to Zeno. In fact, George's confrontation of the central tenets of Logical Positivism functions as a focus in *Jumpers* for Stoppard's continued exploration of the nature of freedom and of criticism and his treatment of the political implications of the dissenting voice which, actively denied the means to talk sense, will, nevertheless, not be silenced.

At the root of George's rejection of the prevailing philosophical temper is his need to believe in God, a belief which automatically puts him onto the defensive. 'There is, presumably,' he muses, 'a calendar date – a *moment* – when the onus of proof passed from the atheist to the believer, when, quite suddenly, secretly, the noes had it' (p. 25). Moore's God is not only a Creator but also the origin and guarantee of absolute values, in morality and aesthetics. However, he insists that his belief in God is not a matter of blind faith; if God exists, he tells us, he certainly did so before religion, that glorified supporters' club. No, if God exists, as George is adamant he does, he 'is a philosopher's God, logically inferred from self-evident premises' (pp. 39–40). Herein lies George's difficulty, and his importance. The spiritual loners of Stoppard's earlier work, as we have seen, associate freedom with refusal, not criticism. George, however, does not refuse the rules of the philosophical language-game, but attempts to stay within them. This is real dissent, the attempt to engage with opponents, to initiate a genuine and fruitful dialogue, to espouse the principle of argument. George's failure is measured by his final inability to transcend these rules, to explode the assumptions of philosophy from within.

George's failure, and the exact nature of his dissent, can only be really understood in the context of his critique of Logical Positivism. The orthodox mainstream against which he swims is made up of 'Logical Positivists, mainly, with a linguistic analyst or two, a couple of Benthamite Utilitarians . . . Lapsed Kantians and empiricists generally . . . and of course the usual Behaviourists . . . a mixture,' he concludes, 'of the more philosophical members of the university gymnastics team and the more gymnastic members of the Philosophy School' (pp. 50–51). In so doing he finds himself in the position of having to display a sensitivity towards the methods of enquiry espoused by his manifold, if unanimous, opponents. The opening of his paper shows the extent to which George must attempt procedures specifically designed for his antagonists' uses. 'To begin at the beginning,' he assures us, 'is God? (Pause) I prefer to put the question in this form because to ask, "Does God exist?" appears to presuppose the existence of a God who may not' (p. 24). George is here hyper-conscious of the argument put forward by Ayer in *Language, Truth and Logic* that our habit of thinking of existence as an attribute was the result of our misunderstanding of our own language, a misunderstanding which encourages us to see sentences such as 'Unicorns are fictitious' as being of the same order and grammatical type as 'Dogs are faithful'.[8] Ayer's point is that it is our superstitious belief that for every word or phrase which can be the grammatical subject of a sentence there must be somewhere a real entity which corresponds to it, which leads us to postulate real non-existent entities – such as unicorns or deities. Russell's attempt to sort out this confused tangle of sentences of differing orders, his Theory of Descriptions, had claimed that it was impossible to assert the existence of individuals, but not of descriptions. ' "Existence", according to this theory,' explains Russell in typically trenchant mood, 'can only be asserted of descriptions. We can say, "The author of *Waverley* exists," but to say "Scott exists" is bad grammar, or rather bad syntax. This clears up two millenia of muddle-headedness about "existence" beginning with Plato's *Theaetatus*.'[9] If this is the case, George refuses to accept it – and Russell's remark is subjected to a fair amount of open ridicule.

George is happy to side with Plato in declaring that existence *is* something of which the mind is aware in objects – no matter what confusions this may throw our syntax into. George has both fun and difficulty with the Theory of Descriptions, a theory which places the demands and witness of our language above those of our intuition. It is ironic, for instance, that George is never quite sure how to describe the author of the theory. 'Do I say, "My friend the late Bertrand Russell," ' he asks his wife, 'or "My late friend Bertrand Russell?" They both sound funny.' 'Probably,' replies Dotty, 'because he wasn't your friend' (p. 31). In the opening section of George's philosophical paper his inability to describe Russell satisfactorily gives rise to a tortured extempore variation on Russell's response to the various claims to existence of Scott and the author of *Waverley*. He begs permission to refer to the late Lord Russell, 'an old friend for whom punctuality was no less a predicate than existence, and a good deal more so, he would have had us believe, though why we should believe that existence could be asserted of the author of *Principia Mathematica* but not of Bertrand Russell, he never had time, despite his punctuality, not to mention his existence, to explain' (p. 25). At pains to explain the central tenets of the philosophy he is denying, George takes an obvious delight in exposing what he considers its comical absurdities. More often than not, his expositions of Logical Positivism can be traced back directly to passages in Ayer's *Language, Truth and Logic*, just as his joke at Russell's expense is a verbal ambush of the passage already quoted from his *History of Western Philosophy*. For instance, George's jibe at his rival McFee, in which he describes him as 'A very good man in his way, though perhaps I should describe him as generally approved of – he doesn't, of course, believe in good and bad as such' (p. 48), is a direct reference to the chapter 'Critique of Ethics and Theology' in *Language, Truth and Logic*, in which Ayer claims that all our statements about value are entirely subjective in being merely expressions of our feelings about objects and draws an important distinction between expressions of feelings about objects and descriptions of feelings about objects. On occasions such as these, George's verbal jokes win the point for him – but on other occasions it is he who is ambushed by language. This is when it is most painfully obvious that the procedures of proof and exposition have been laid out in front of him, that the vehicle of the critique has been appropriated by his opponents. George's verbal squirmings teeter dangerously on the brink of gibberish.

He has, for instance, a disastrous encounter with that capstone of the Logical Positivist philosophy, the Verification Principle. Dotty provides the best introduction to the problem when she recites the Gospel according to Sir Archibald Jumper. 'Things and actions, you understand,' she intones, 'can have any number of real and verifiable properties. But good and bad, better and worse, these are not real properties of things, they are just expressions of our feelings about them.' George's response is one of scepticism: 'Archie says' (p. 41). As presented by Ayer, the outcome of this supposition is that we can only make significant statements about those properties which we can verify. A statement is only meaningful if we know what empirical observations would prove its truth or falsehood. If we cannot think of a method to prove or disprove a statement then it is of no significance, has no meaning, is, literally, nonsense. This argument (or, rather, pre-empting of argument) is of particular significance to George Moore in his protracted consideration of the objectivity of moral judgements and the necessity of a divine First Cause. The consequence of Ayer's argument with regard to both moral and aesthetic value-judgements is to deny that there can be any debate about them, that in speaking of them we can talk anything but nonsense. When we say that something is 'wrong', according to Ayer, we are not saying anything about that action itself, we are merely reacting in a certain way to that action. Nor are we describing our feelings because that would be to make a verifiable statement; if I said 'that's wrong', my statement could be verified by a man looking into my mind, or heart, to see if I really disapproved. He could contradict my statement, could assert its falsehood by saying to me 'You approve of that action'. For Ayer, value-statements do not work in even so radically subjective a manner; they are not verifiable descriptions of a subject's reactions but the very fibre of those reactions, concrete and thus nonsensical expressions of subjectivity. No two value-statements can contradict each other because both are nonsense; Ayer's vision of ethics is of a world emptied of meaning and hence of argument. 'In saying that a certain type of action is right or wrong,' he explains, 'I am not making any factual statement, not even a statement about my own state of mind. I am merely expressing certain moral sentiments. And the man who is ostensibly contradicting me is merely expressing his moral sentiments. So there is plainly no sense in arguing which of us is in the right. For neither of us is asserting a genuine proposition.'[10]

For George, the Verification Principle is Catch–22, a lethal trap carefully laid by the Logical Positivists. Not only can George not disagree over ethical statements and ethical absolutes, because anything he has to say about them is nonsensical and hence incapable of contradiction, he cannot make statements about God, the necessary guarantor of his absolutes, because that would also be to make an unverifiable and hence metaphysical and nonsensical proposition. Ayer is characteristically truculent on this point; he describes the mystic as someone who believes that God exists but is unable to express his knowledge in significant (that is, empirically testable) statements. 'It is no use his saying that he has apprehended facts but is unable to express them,' says Ayer of the mystic, 'For we know that if he really had acquired any information, he would be able to express it. He would be able to indicate in some way or other how the genuineness of his discovery might be empirically determined. The fact that he cannot reveal what he "knows", or even himself devise an empirical test to validate his "knowledge" shows that his state of mystical intuition is not a genuinely cognitive state.'[11] George is all too conscious of this criticism. There is no empirical means of testing his claims and, consequently, no way of bending language to his purposes and making significant statements. Despising the leap to religious faith, George's search for the philosopher's God is rendered futile before it has begun. His attempts to wriggle out of the trap become increasingly tortured and ineffective. 'All I know,' he proffers, 'is that I think that I know that nothing can be created out of nothing, that my moral conscience is different from the rules of my tribe, and that there is more in me than meets the microscope – and because of *that* I'm lumbered with this incredible and definitely shifty *God*, the dog-eared trump-card of atheism' (p. 68). This motif is repeated, and George's confusion increases perceptibly; he finds himself relinquishing 'Knowledge', he admits defeat in the linguistic battle for the word and accepts the definition thrust upon him by the Logical Positivists. 'How does one know what it is one believes,' he asks, casting himself in the role of Ayer's bemused mystic with whom argument is simply a waste of breath, 'when it is so difficult to know what it is one knows? I don't claim to *know* that God exists, I only claim that he does without my knowing it, and while I claim as much I do not claim to know as much; indeed I cannot know and God knows I cannot' (p. 71). The supreme irony of George's encounter with the Verification Principle is that in laying claim to an intuitive apprehension of the truth he makes a massive blunder. At the very moment when he stands up most volubly against the Verification Principle George is, quite glaringly, wrong. 'There are many things I know,' he insists, 'which are not verifiable but nobody can tell me I don't know them, and I think that I know that something happened to poor Dotty and she somehow killed McFee, as sure as she killed my poor Thumper' (p. 78). The play never quite resolves the question of who killed McFee. What we do know is that Dotty did not kill Thumper: George did, accidentally impaling the hare on the arrow unleashed to prove the absurdity of Zeno's paradox and the necessity of a First Cause.

George is constantly betrayed by language, the paramount importance of which his whole philosophical position is an attempt to deny. Language, he tells us, is a finite instrument crudely applied to the infinity of his ideas, yet for his philosophical rivals it has become the most important field of legitimate enquiry. In seeking to demonstrate the central Logical Positivist claim that all statements about value are nonsense and that all debate about it can never rise above the level of mere abuse, McFee, George's immediate philosophical rival, devotes himself to the exhaustive listing of linguistic oddities designed to display the range of contradictory uses to which statements about value are put. His aim, as described scathingly by George, is to show that the word 'good' has meant 'different things to different people at different times, an exercise which combines simplicity with futility in a measure he does not apparently suspect, for on the one hand it is not a statement which anyone would dispute and on the other, nothing useful can be inferred from it. It is not,' he adds, 'in fact a statement about value at all; it is a statement about language and how it is used in a particular society. Nevertheless, up this deeply-rutted garden path, Professor McFee leads us, pointing out items of interest along the way' (p. 54). The irony of George's criticisms is that he constantly finds the infinity of his ideas denied by the finite tool. 'Though my convictions are intact and my ideas coherent,' he explains to Bones, 'I can't seem to find the words . . . .' Ignoring the Inspector's observation that 'Are God?' is wrong for a start, George adds that 'the words betray the thoughts they are supposed to express. Even the most generalized truth begins to look like special pleading as soon as you trap it in language' (p. 46).

Bennett claims that the relationship between the jokes in *Jumpers* and their philosophical material is often verbal and superficial.[12] In fact, the verbal play has a function: to show that in combating the orthodox mainstream emphasis on linguistic analysis, George has lost control of language. Tripped up by language in his contest with the Verification Principle, George is similarly incommoded when arguing against Russell's proposition that the series of proper fractions is an example of a sequence which does not have a first term and, by implication, cause. 'But the fact is,' counters George, lapsing into an absurdity which effectively negates the point he is striving to make, 'the first term is not an infinite fraction, but *zero*. It exists. God, so to speak, is nought' (p. 29). Trapped by language, his conviction indeed looks like special pleading. Later Dotty points out that George's attempts to wrestle serviceable terms from the grasp of his philosophical opponents amounts to a preoccupation with language-puzzles which prevents him from initiating any meaningful action. During his period of passionate intimacy with Dotty somebody else bagged the title of his would-be masterpiece *The Concept of Knowledge*. 'He'd stolen a march,' points out Dotty, 'while you were still comparing knowledge in the sense of having-experience-of, with knowledge in the sense of being-acquainted-with, and knowledge in the sense of inferring facts with knowledge in the sense of comprehending truths, and all the time as you got more and more acquainted with, though no more comprehending of, the symbolic patterns on my Persian carpet, it was knowing in the biblical sense of screwing that you were learning about and maybe there's a book in you yet – '(p. 36). Nor is it only in the field of academic philosophy that George finds himself at the mercy of the pun. His linguistic incompetence is continually contrasted with the verbal gymnastics of the philosophical and political jumpers. Having established language as a focus of attention they can make it do whatever they want. Language jumps along with the rest of them. 'Are you telling me,' George asks Dotty, incredulously, 'that the Radical Liberal spokesman for Agriculture has been made Archbishop of Canterbury?!!' 'Don't shout at me,' she replies, 'I suppose if you think of him as a sort of . . . shepherd, ministering to his flock . . .' (p. 38). Dotty goes on to suggest that the old Archbishop uncoped himself. 'Dis-mantled himself, perhaps' (p. 38) suggests George, bitterly acknowledging the pre-eminence of the pun in the new world beyond the luxury confines of his Mayfair flat.

George's dissenting voice is muffled by his inability to kick himself free from language. The method and medium of philosophical discourse are prescribed for him; George is enough of a Logical Positivist to accept that philosophy must display and adhere to a rigorous syntax of its own, and he makes himself ridiculous by attempting to order his intuitions according to that syntax. In searching for his philosopher's God, George fails to redefine what philosophy is; it remains a finite instrument crudely applied to the infinity of his ideas. His failure to criticise – to both *engage* with and free himself from – the procedures and assumptions of his opponents measures his own responsibility for his shortcomings as a spiritual dissident, shortcomings that Stoppard makes obvious in the relationship between his fictional George Moore and the historical G. E. Moore, the Cambridge philosopher described by Ayer, in his introduction to *Language, Truth and Logic*, as one of the founding-fathers of the new school of linguistic analysis.

George's philosophical position and method of argument owe much to those of G. E. Moore, and suffer the same fate. Both are ethical intuitionists for whom 'good' is an actual property possessed by things in this world. As G. E. Moore puts it in *Principia Ethica*, anyone thinking of 'intrinsic value' or 'intrinsic worth', 'has before his mind the unique object – the unique property of things – which I mean by "good".'[13] Man as subject is an intuitive being who cannot be dragged into the dock for breach of the Principle of Verification. This emphasis on the reality of intuitive recognition has two important extensions – in G. E. Moore's theory of ethics and his theory of knowledge. In the first place, he conceives of ethics as meta-ethics, a study of ethical assertions. By a detailed analytic study of the many different ways in which 'good' is used, Moore claims to have discovered that there is only one primary meaning of 'good', that is, 'good in itself'.[14] 'Good' is thus Moore's basic ethical term and the basic ethical question is, 'What is good?'. Secondly, Moore's theory of knowledge rests on a thoroughgoing defence of common-sense. He maintains the truth and certainty of a number of very general propositions making up what he called the commonsense view of the world. Among these propositions are the assertions of the existence of material objects and acts of consciousness, but not, unfortunately for Stoppard's Moore, of God. The crux of G. E. Moore's position was that he need advance no arguments in favour of these propositions – indeed, he *could* not. While claiming he knew certain propositions to be true, he gladly admitted not knowing *how* he knew them to be true. G. E. Moore has successfully appropriated the word 'knowledge'; Stoppard's Moore can only reach a botched compromise with the empiricists, drawing a linguistically paraplegic distinction between claims, which he makes, and knowledge, which he admits he cannot have. George cannot follow his predecessor without admitting the futility of his search for the philosopher's God, logically inferred from self-evident premises.

However, despite not being able to wrest 'knowledge' from his enemies, George goes a long way in following the intuitionist argument. He too makes 'good' the basis of his ethics. 'What can be said to be the impulse of a genuinely altruistic act?' asks George, pondering the appalling incident on the moon in which astronaut Oates is left behind by Captain Scott and the crippled spacecraft, 'Hobbes might have answered self-esteem, but what is the attraction or point in thinking better of oneself? What is better?' (p. 55). In considering this basic ethical question George is adamant that 'good' is indefinable, that its primary meaning cannot be analysed into a meaning of another order. Good, he maintains, is knowable, but not nameable. 'It is not nameable,' he explains, 'because it is not another way of referring to this or that quality we have decided is virtuous: It is not courage, and it is not honesty or loyalty or kindness. The irreducible fact of goodness is not implicit in any one kind of action more than in its opposite, but in the existence of a relationship between the two. It is the sense of comparisons being in order' (p. 55). G. E. Moore had described attempts to subsume 'good' under concepts of another order as the Naturalistic Fallacy, the consequence of which would be to destroy the unique character of 'good' and ethics as an autonomous branch of philosophical enquiry. For George, however, the attempt to avoid the Naturalistic Fallacy has dangerous repercussions of its own.

The irony of George Moore's relationship with his historical predecessor is most apparent in his handling of the commonsense argument. 'Here is one hand, here is another,' announced G. E. Moore in his lecture *Proof of an External World* as a response to Kant's claim that it was a scandal to philosophy that the existence of things outside us must be accepted on faith alone.[15] George has similar recourse to practical demonstration in his refutation of Zeno; commonsense will make a mockery of Zeno's claim that an arrow cannot reach its target, nor indeed leave the bow and that 'Saint Sebastian died of fright' (p. 28). The larger point of the exercise is to combat Russell's dismissal of the First Cause argument. Distracted by an outlandish scream from Dotty, George looses the arrow prematurely and it wings its way over the wardrobe to disappear from sight. We are presented with a grisly answer to the question, 'Who killed Thumper?'. Discovering the hare impaled on his arrow and staggered by his complicity in the crime of which he had accused Dotty, George steps onto his hapless pet tortoise. In attempting his commonsense proof of the necessity of the Creator, George has become an unnecessary Destroyer.

'A certain amount of professional name-dropping occurs,' writes Bennett, pursuing his claim that the play's philosophy is 'flaunted' rather than functional, 'but all Stoppard does with the names is to drop them.'[16] George would do well to drop his name if he could; it functions, in fact, as an index of the power of language in the world of *Jumpers*. George is incapacitated by the Cognomen Syndrome: G. E. Moore's methods of demonstration have rounded on him. He is well aware of the poignancy in his inheritance of the illustrious name. 'It is ironic,' he explains, 'that the school which denies the claims of the intuition to know good when it sees it, is itself the product of the pioneer work set out in his *Principia Ethica* by the late G. E. Moore, an intuitionist philosopher whom I respected from afar but who, for reasons which will be found adequate by logical spirits, was never in when I called' (p. 67). G. E. Moore's emphasis on the need to analyse ethical statements back to primary meanings indirectly refocused the interests of philosophy; his successors took their lead not from his faith in the intuition but from the analytic methods by which Moore hoped to prove the indefinability of 'good'. His own methods helped to establish language as the sole means and end of philosophical disquisition. Moore's insistence upon the indefinability of 'good', his guarantee of ethics as an autonomous branch of philosophy, also has serious consequences for George. Archie's dismissal of George's claims to the now vacant Chair of Logic is symptomatic of the inferior status of ethics in the world of the Jumpers. As long as George's belief in God can be described as ethical, instead of logical, his protestations can be of no threat to a society whose smooth running depends on the judicious espousal of expediency. '*Your* strong point is, how shall I put it,' explains Archie, 'well, many of the students are under the impression that you are the author of *Principia Ethica*' (p. 73). The remark serves to emphasise the peripheral position which George occupies; as long as he is hampered with the word 'ethical' he will remain, 'our tame believer, pointed out to visitors in much the same spirit as we point out the magnificent stained glass in what is now the gymnasium' (p. 63). George's insistence that his belief in God *is* logical gives his enemies all the ammunition they need. 'Logic' has been appropriated by the Logical Positivists; by using the word George is inviting his opponents to invoke the Verification Principle. 'In a wholly rational society,' acknowledges George, recognising the status of bemused mystic to which he is thus condemned, 'the moralist will be a variety of crank, haranguing the bus queue with the demented certitude of one blessed with privileged information – "Good and evil are metaphysical absolutes!" ' (p. 40). Metaphysical, unverifiable statements, the Logical Positivists tell us, *mean* nothing. George is not even worth arguing with.

For Logical Positivism there is, Ayer claims, no need, or even possibility, of rival philosophical schools; any problem which Logical Postivism cannot solve is a 'fictitious problem, since all genuine problems are at least theoretically capable of being solved'.[17] The prevailing philosophical temper is, George discovers, self-sealed against all possibility of criticism; his struggle is that of a man attempting dissent where none is possible. On the debit side, however, George's revolt is qualified by his propensity to draw a circle around philosophy. Despite his proud boast that were he given the Chair of Logic, it would 'apply itself occasionally to the activities of the human race' (p. 73), he is all too prone to thinking of himself as a philosopher first and a citizen second. His detached disapproval of the world outside philosophy and his flat is a constantly recurring theme. He recalls trying to discuss the Theory of Descriptions with Bertrand Russell (who, incidentally, was attempting to contact Chairman Mao through the local exchange with the wine-waiter from the Pagoda Garden hanging on to interpret); Dotty remembers George rambling on about 'Language being the aniseed trail that draws the hounds of heaven when the metaphysical fox has gone to earth', and he is stung into defending himself. 'I was simply trying to bring his mind back to matters of universal import,' he replies, 'and away from the day-to-day parochialism of international politics.' '*Universal import!*' gasps Dotty, 'You're living in dreamland!' (p. 31). Later, when Inspector Bones asks him what he was doing during the fatal party to celebrate the Radical Liberal victory at the polls, George says, 'I'm not interested in politics. I was trying to write my paper' (pp. 47–48). As a philosopher George is painfully aware that language has been appropriated by a collective interest, as a man he refuses to acknowledge the radical political consequences such an appropriation must entail.

In claiming that there is no structural relationship between the philosophy and the rest of the play, Bennett fails to recognise the way that the philosophical discussion is used to engage, at the level of content, the same problem as the play addresses at the level of form. In essence, *Jumpers* succeeds where George fails. George cannot free himself from philosophical procedures designed to prevent him saying what he wants to say, but we have already seen how *Jumpers* observes procedure only to transcend it and how, again unlike George, it performs an act of criticism that is genuinely creative: it proclaims its own nature by demonstrating and departing from the disciplines of the literary materials at its disposal. To return to Bennett: the relationship between the philosophy and the rest of the play can be seen in the very *structure* of *Jumpers*, which (as a critical engagement with those alternatives which appear to be available to it) is a corrective to George's ill-fated struggle to find his own voice. In other words, Stoppard uses the academic philosophical material less to illuminate the question of absolute values in morality and aesthetics than to make a more general point about the possibility, and the difficulty, of earning freedom through the performance of criticism. In the group of plays we shall now turn to Stoppard creates dissenting voices which, unlike George, acknowledge, and engage with, the political nature of that struggle.

6

The Dissidents

'In the end,' Professor Anderson is assured by Pavel Hollar in
Professional Foul, 'it must change. But I have something to say –
that is all. If I leave my statement behind, then it's O.K. You
understand?'[1] Having something to say, the dissidents of *Every Good
Boy Deserves Favour*, *Professional Foul* and *Dogg's Hamlet,
Cahoot's Macbeth* are involved in a political struggle for language;
their problem is to construct an alternative language in which to
make their statements – a means of expression capable of criticising
the assumptions and propositions of the Communist state. In *Dogg's
Hamlet, Cahoot's Macbeth* Stoppard's examination of the nature of
political criticism occasions a radical realignment of his 'spiritual
loners': dissent is recognised not as a solitary condition but as a
genuinely effective group activity.

The gala performance of *Every Good Boy Deserves Favour* at the
John Player Centenary Festival in July 1977 had a mixed reception
from its critics. In the *Daily Telegraph*, for instance, John Barber
voiced his outrage at the presumptuousness of the author who had
assembled an eighty-strong orchestra on stage in order to tell a
simple story of political oppression the sentiments of which (Barber
assumed) nobody could possibly fail to share.[2] Bernard Levin, on
the other hand, described the play as an enhancement of 'civilisation
itself' and, amid a welter of allusion to de la Mare, Chesterton,
Beethoven and Shaw, extolled Stoppard's *saeva indignatio* which
'still holding laughter by the hand cuts deeper and deeper weals into
the body of the wickedness he seeks to depict.'[3] In the *Guardian*
Michael Billington was less ecstatic, but complimentary nonetheless.
The play, he felt, flouted the theatrical law which says, 'you cannot
have your hand on your heart and your tongue in your cheek at the
same time'. He went on to explain that Stoppard here combined
'tonic verbal playfulness with a palpable social conscience'.[4]
However, Billington's remarks need to be qualified: in *Every Good
Boy Deserves Favour* Stoppard does not simply append a new

111

element (social comment) to his characteristic linguistic 'clownery'. To be precise, his puns *enact* the politics of control.

The most significant pun occurs in an exchange between Alexander Ivanov, the dissident, and the Doctor, who insists on denying the claim that sane people are being locked up in mental institutions. 'I have a complaint,' announced Alexander. 'Yes, I know – ' comes the reply, 'pathological development of the personality with paranoid delusions' (p. 26).[5] One language runs up against another. The dissident's problem is that the very cogency of his convictions will be enough to condemn both them and him; unlike George Moore, he *can* find the words but this is a world in which the speaker is in the power of the listener. The Doctor cites the parallel case of Pyotr Grigorenko 'of whom it has been stated by our leading psychiatrists at the Serbsky Institute, that his outwardly well adjusted behaviour and formally coherent utterances were indicative of a pathological development of the personality' (pp. 30–31). The Doctor notes that 'Your disease is dissent. Your kind of schizophrenia does not presuppose changes of personality noticeable to others' (p. 30). So, Alexander's views are consigned to nonsense as effectively as George Moore's metaphysical intuitions; like the Logical Positivists of *Jumpers*, the Doctor, and the authorities he represents, are self-sealed against criticism.

Significantly, the man for Alexander's case is Colonel (or, rather, Doctor) Rozinsky, whose speciality, the Doctor explains, is semantics: 'He's a Doctor of Philology, whatever that means. I'm told he's a genius' (p. 28). Indeed, it is the authorities' control over meaning and language (in a sense, the very adroitness of the ways they listen) which allows them to save face when it becomes clear that Alexander Ivanov will not be broken and admit his insanity: the fact that his name is the same as his mad cell-mate with the imaginary orchestra allows Rozinsky to choose which of them to listen to. Alexander states, quite truthfully, that he does *not* have an orchestra, his cure is proclaimed and he is released without embarrassing the authorities by dying in their custody.

Every Good Boy Deserves Favour is a flawed play, most noticeably in its attempt to construct for the dissident an alternative language. Faced with the manic verbal gyrations of his lunatic cell-mate ('I've got a tubercular great-nephew of John Philip Sousa who goes oom when he should be going pah. And the Jew's harp has applied for a visa,' (p. 17)) and the intransigence of the Doctor, Alexander resorts to humdrum rhyming mnemonics which he hopes will preserve his convictions, as in amber, for his son, Sacha. Stoppard is here treading a dangerous path, aiming for a stark simplicity to carry the emotional weight of his support for the dissident. Although the device works at the level of analogy – linking with those scenes in which mnemonics have been used by the Teacher and the Doctor to push a view onto Sacha and Ivanov – it too often betrays the play into bathos: 'Dear Sacha, try to see/what they call their liberty/is just the freedom to agree,' recites Alexander, 'that one and one is sometimes three./I kiss you now, remember me./Don't neglect your geometry' (pp. 34–5). Nevertheless, the play is, in terms of Stoppard's development, an important piece, a demonstration of political realities as the collision of discourse with discourse. It also raises many of the questions which Stoppard explores with rather greater success in the television play *Professional Foul*.

Professional Foul was suggested by a trip Stoppard made to Russia in 1977 to collect signatures protesting against the Soviet treatment of dissidents.[6] He found himself the victim of a professional foul by the Soviet Customs Officers, who simply stole the document. This visit to Moscow unlocked for Stoppard his first play about Czechoslovakia where he had been born and which his family fled on the eve of the Nazi invasion. Ronald Hayman claims that 'if the BBC had presented the play pseudonymously, it would have been identifiable as Stoppard's work only by virtue of a few sequences'.[7] In fact, it is very much the genuine article. Not only does the play pick up where *Every Good Boy Deserves Favour* left off, in Professor Anderson it introduces a character who is recognisably descended from George Moore, but who does not persist in a facile separation of philosophy and politics. Once again language is at the very centre of the play as Stoppard focuses on the battles we do for it and the misunderstandings and absurdities into which it can betray us.

Philosophy and football provide, of course, the most obvious clash of contexts setting discourse against discourse. Attending the Prague Colloquium mainly in order to see the World Cup qualifying game between England and Czechoslovakia, Anderson is more at home talking about soccer than philosophy, particularly linguistic philosophy. Unfortunately, many of his pearls of footballing wisdom are cast before the uncomprehending McKendrick, a social scientist with fashionable left-wing views and a bluff manner. 'He's what used to be called left-wing,' says Anderson of Crisp. 'Broadbent's in the centre. He's an opportunist more than anything' (p. 50). McKendrick hangs on his every word, eager for inside information on his philosophical colleagues (or, rather, rivals). The confusion reaches its crisis when McKendrick confronts two of the England party in the lift, and accosts them with his customary brusqueness; 'Bill McKendrick, I hear you're doing some very interesting work in Newcastle. Great stuff. I like to think of myself as a bit of a left-winger at Stoke. Of course, my stuff is largely empirical – I leave epistemological questions to the scholastics – eh, Anderson?' (pp. 59–60). Anderson winces, McKendrick prattles on about neo-Hegelians and Quinian neo-Positivists and the two footballers find themselves in as much need of a simultaneous translation as will the assembled philosophers at the multi-national colloquium.

In the exchanges between Anderson and his ex-student Hollar the clash of discourses is given a more poignant treatment. Trying to persuade Anderson to smuggle out of the country his politically contentious thesis, Hollar tells him that he is now working as a cleaner:

> ANDERSON: (*with intelligent interest*) A cleaner? What is that?
> HOLLAR: (*surprised*) Cleaning. Washing. With a brush and a bucket. I am a cleaner at the bus station.
> ANDERSON: You wash buses?
> HOLLAR: No, not buses – the lavatories, the floors where people walk and so on.
> ANDERSON: Oh. I see. You're a *cleaner*.
>
> (p. 52)

Hollar is experiencing the same painful problem as Alexander Ivanov: he is another speaker in the power of his listener. As Anderson is drawn into discussing Hollar's thesis the struggle between competing discourses becomes even more marked. Hollar's basic contention is that the State must be judged ethically against the fundamental ethic of the individual, but he admits that this is not safe. 'Quite,' responds Anderson, 'The difficulty arises when one asks oneself how the *individual* ethic can have any meaning by itself. Where does *that* come from? In what sense is it intelligible, for example, to say that a man has certain inherent, individual rights?' (p. 55). His discourse changes gear from the philosophical to the pedagogical: 'I only mean it is a question you will have to deal with.' Hollar's answer is quiet, and crushing: 'I mean, it is not safe for me' (p. 55). The point is clear: safety is one thing for a professional philosopher painstakingly constructing an argument on logical inference and self-evident premises, it is another for a cleaner who concludes that there is an obligation, a human responsibility to fight against State correctness.

Despite being made, on occasions, to look ridiculous, as here, Anderson is distinguished by his deepening awareness of the political implications of his philosophical position, and of the complexity of political action. From the beginning he shares George Moore's contempt for the nit-picking of linguistic analysis: 'A lot of chaps pointing out that we don't always mean what we say, even when we manage to say what we mean' (p. 44). He admits to collecting oddities for the language chaps: 'It's like handing round a bag of licorice allsorts. They're terribly grateful' (p. 45). Yet he himself, at this stage, is not above a bit of word-spinning. He refuses, for instance, to tell McKendrick about his ulterior motives for attending the Colloquium: 'You see, if I tell you I make you a co-conspirator whether or not you would have wished to be one. Ethically I should give you the opportunity of choosing to be one or not' (p. 47). Anderson has constructed a neat impasse – he cannot give McKendrick the choice without pre-empting it. It is all so many words, with the great secret nothing more than his intention to go to the football match. Later, of course, Anderson will be faced with a real choice between telling McKendrick about the thesis, or simply hiding it in his colleague's luggage. In the end he hides it and makes what is by his own admission an ethical imposition – of the very kind he had warned Hollar he would be making should Hollar hide the thesis in Anderson's own luggage.

Central to an understanding of Anderson's shifting position is the scene in which he attempts to sidle out of the Colloquium and is, instead, trapped into delivering an impromptu riposte to the speaker, Stone. We have already seen in a series of close-ups – one of the television play's most telling sequences – the bewilderment of the audience, and of the simultaneous translators they are listening to, as the American Professor gives a tortured analysis of the subtle difference between 'The show ran well on Broadway', and 'Native Dancer ran well at Kentucky'. Forced into some sort of observation, Anderson opens, casually, by turning the tables on language analysis in general, and Logical Positivism in particular. 'Whereof we cannot speak,' he notes, edging closer to the exit, 'thereof we are by no means silent' (p. 63). In so doing, he travesties the ending of Wittgenstein's *Tractatus Logico-Philosophicus*. For the Wittgenstein of the 'Tractatus', the limits of language constituted the limits of the world.

The forms of language could be analysed back to a single predomi-
nant form, a direct linguistic transcription of objective reality: what
could not be contained in language could not exist in the world.[8] So
central an emphasis on the importance of language proved a seminal
insight for the Logical Positivists, and in denying it Anderson is
knocking away the fundamental support for their position.[9] He insists
that the importance of language is overrated: 'the important truths
are simple and monolithic. The essentials of a given situation speak
for themselves, and language is as capable of obscuring the truth as
of revealing it. Thank you' (p. 63). Ironically, in the panic and
confusion of Hollar's flat, surrounded by police shouting abuse in a
language he does not understand, Anderson will find his glib assurance put to the test. The scene is also a pointed reversal of that in
his hotel when Anderson had consistently misheard Hollar despite
the fact that both were speaking the *same* language. His understanding of what takes place when the Czech police claim to find the
foreign currency prompts not only his decision to change the paper
he had agreed to read but also his smuggling of Hollar's thesis out
of the country. Educated by experience, Anderson learns that the
dissident cannot simply 'speak for himself'.

For McKendrick the philosophical position which Anderson
nonchalantly hints at as he covers his retreat from the hall is something of 'a funk'. 'You're a worse case than Chetwyn and his primitive
Greeks,' is his verdict: 'At least he has the excuse of *believing* in
goodness and beauty. You know they're fictions but you're so hung
up on them you want to treat them as if they were God-given
absolutes' (p. 78). For McKendrick, then, *Ethical Fictions as Ethical
Foundations* is something of a professional foul, a calculated, though
strictly-speaking 'non-legitimate', gambit which allows Anderson to
avoid the consequences of his position: he can speak of the importance of moral absolutes without incurring the charge of being a
mystic. This becomes explicit later when he addresses the Colloquium. He claims that ethics are the inspiration of our behaviour
and not merely the creation of our utterances: 'We must see that
natural justice, however illusory, does inspire many people's behaviour much of the time. As an ethical utterance it does seem to be
an attempt to define a sense of rightness which is not simply derived
from some other utterance elsewhere' (p. 90). This paper is a
professional foul in an additional and important sense; the title is
the same as that approved by the Colloquium authorities, but
Anderson has changed its application to lend his voice to Hollar's.

He seeks to show that rules are a secondary and consequential elaboration of rights, 'and I will be associating rules generally with communities and rights generally with individuals' (p. 87). While acknowledging that these rights *are* fictions he concludes that 'there is an obligation to treat them as if they were truths' (p. 87). From this platform he launches a radical criticism of the Czech State's violation of individual (though, of course, fictitious) rights – a criticism which his original paper had not made. The Colloquium authorities react in kind. By emptying the hall with a fire-alarm they commit a professional foul of their own.

However, perhaps the most important of the professional fouls is that committed by Anderson on McKendrick. 'It's not quite playing the game is it?' (p. 93) gasps McKendrick when Anderson's subterfuge becomes apparent. This deliberate infringement of the rules of the game (by Anderson's own definition the hiding of the thesis in his fellow-traveller's luggage is an unethical act) lends significance to McKendrick's own outline of the Catastrophe Theory. The crux of what he says is that, according to this theory, Morality and Immorality are not parallel lines that never meet, but two edges of the same plane. Twisted into the catastrophe curve, this plane produces a model of behaviour in the real world: 'There's a point – the catastrophe point – where your progress along one line of behaviour jumps you into the opposite line; the principle reverses itself at the point where a rational man would abandon it' (p. 79). There are, then, no moral principles, just a lot of principled people acting as if there were. McKendrick's articulate and dispassionate critique opposes the complexities of experience to the monolithic simplicities of belief, and elicits a rather grudging admission from Anderson. 'You're right up to a point,' he says, 'There would be no moral dilemmas if moral principles worked in straight lines and never crossed each other' (p. 79). As he discovers Anderson's stratagem, McKendrick witnesses his ideas reach their own catastrophe point when they jump, rather painfully for him, from theory to reality. 'Last night,' offers Anderson, 'I'm afraid I reversed a principle'(p. 93).

Anderson discovers that the important truths are *not* simple and monolithic: his professional foul recognises a set of problems rather than ready-made options. 'Ethics,' he assures the shaken McKendrick as their plane taxies, 'is a very complicated business. That's why we have these congresses' (p. 93). The irony is clear and recalls the earlier exchange about the Catastrophe Theory in which

Anderson has admitted that in matters ethical, 'One meets test situations which have troubled much cleverer men than us.' 'A good rule, I find,' replies Chetwyn, 'is to try them out on men much less clever than us. I often ask my son what *he* thinks' (p. 79). In his paper at the Colloquium Anderson returns to this intuitionist argument. He admits that a philosopher exploring the difficult terrain of right and wrong should not be over-impressed with the argument that a child would know the difference, 'But when, let us say, we are being persuaded that it is ethical to put someone in prison for reading or writing the wrong books, it is well to be reminded that you can persuade a man to believe almost anything provided he is clever enough, but it is much more difficult to persuade someone less clever' (p. 90). He drives a wedge, here, between intellect and emotion in the same way as *Professional Foul* itself. The audience's intuitive recognition of an ethical act in Anderson's hiding of the thesis is cancelled by his own objections and by his insistence that ethics is a matter of recognising problems rather than simply relying on solutions. In other words, the play avoids the sentimentalism of *Every Good Boy Deserves Favour;* instead of enlisting its audience *Professional Foul* attempts to *engage* with them. As a naturalistic television play (and here we should recall Stoppard's comments about the appeal of 'unnaturalistic' things happening on *stage*, a consideration which determines the respective forms of *Jumpers* and the television play from which it is developed) this engagement can take place at the level of content only and is, therefore, provisional and mediated.

In *Dogg's Hamlet, Cahoot's Macbeth*, however, Stoppard returns to the formal exuberance of the earlier stage plays. In the first half of the play, by staging a language-game from Wittgenstein's *Philosophical Investigations*, Stoppard attempts to teach a new language to the audience. This element of engagement is heightened in the second half when the bizarre proceedings (which have included crude slapstick and the staging of a ravaged Shakespearean text) are suddenly transposed into a new and menacing context. Philosophical parlour-game and mildly diverting stage-business are given a critically new aspect. *Dogg's Hamlet, Cahoot's Macbeth* evinces, in this sense, the same intention as *Travesties:* both show Stoppard's desire to ambush his audience's assumptions about the kind of play they are watching.

The opening section (a conflation of two plays previously written for Ed Berman's Inter-Action Group, *The Fifteen Minute Hamlet* and *Dogg's Our Pet*) is a demonstration of the central tenet of *Philosophical Investigations* – that language is not a calculus logically inferred from the grid-pattern of reality but a form of life, a communal activity capable of change and growth. Indeed, the play shows Stoppard's discovery in *Philosophical Investigations* of ideas and tools which meet his needs as a dramatist, as well as some which deny them. First, the form of language analysis that is practised and recommended in *Philosophical Investigations* is an advance from that of *Tractatus Logico-Philosophicus*. Language is no longer to be analysed back, through a hierarchy of forms, to the reality it transposes. Language is now itself the primal reality; because it has no external support language is not reduced in analysis but laid bare. Analysis displays the manifold language-forms which have become so entwined and knotted that the whole has acquired a prodigious internal strength. Meaning, for the later Wittgenstein, is defined not by an appeal beyond language: it is identified quite squarely with use. Language is a public activity and understanding is defined accordingly as the applicational knowledge of certain operative conventions. Wittgenstein insists, as a consequence, that language can never be private, that it exists solely by virtue of its public presence. Such conclusions would appear to deny the strivings of the spiritual loner or dissident in their attempt to make language susceptible to private initiative: private intention and conviction are ever smothered by the public form of language.

There are, however, other implications to *Philosophical Investigations*. Wittgenstein claims that no discourse is inherently 'realistic' in the sense of being a simple transposition of a state of affairs beyond it. Indeed, freed from any obligation to exterior supports, language becomes alive, capable of change. *Philosophical Investigations* is full of reminders of this obvious fact about language – that it is a continual process of renewal and formation. There are, Wittgenstein tells us, *countless* different kinds of sentences, and 'this multiplicity is not something fixed, given once for all; but new types of language, new language-games, as we may say, come into existence, and others become obsolete and get forgotten.'[10] Pursuing this analogy between language-forms and the games we play he points to the case where we make up the rules as we go along, and 'there is even one where we can alter them – as we go along.'[11]

Wittgenstein's insistence that no single language-form, or collection of rules, is guaranteed by external support parallels Stoppard's that language can be appropriated as a means of criticism. The possibility of dissent as a way of life with its own language – making up the rules, perhaps, as it goes along – becomes real. From this angle Wittgenstein's declaration of the impossibility of a private language looks rather different. When he says this he means that no language is necessarily *unteachable*, that no language is learnt simply by a process of introspection matched with ostensive definition. The language of dissent must, then, be a group activity: a form of life and a means of expression capable of being learned by others. (Just, in fact, as it is learnt by Anderson.) Language as dissent can be caught, learnt in a flash: 'And this is just what we say we do. That is to say: we sometimes describe what we do in these words. But there is nothing astonishing, nothing queer, about what happens.'[12] *Dogg's Hamlet, Cahoot's Macbeth* is about learning in a flash, about spontaneous dissent and the fitting of words to the requirements of a form of life.

The second half of the play presents us with the attempts of a group of dissident actors to perform a truncated version of *Macbeth* which, for the assembled audience, in portraying a brutal and illegal seizure of power, is a reflection of what has happened in Czechoslovakia. For the dissidents the crowning of Malcolm is both an assertion of hope and an affirmation of faith in the efficacy of criticism. The proceedings are constantly interrupted by the Inspector (a sinister development of Stoppard's earlier comic detectives, owing much to Orton's Truscott) who attempts to appropriate both the text and the performance by ending it at the crowning of Macbeth and lauding it with his ominous banalities: 'Very good. Very good! And so nice to have a play with a happy ending for a change.'[13] Stoppard's audience have already picked up some Dogg-language before the interval as they follow the attempts of the lorry-driver, Easy, to make sense of the strange world he has wandered into. In the end, Easy learns Dogg for the specific purpose of abusing the authoritarian headmaster of the boys' school. His entrance in the second half, as he blunders into the action and confuses himself with Banquo's ghost, gives the troupe the chance to use Dogg to finish their performance of *Macbeth* in spite of the Inspector's intrusive presence.

The Inspector is a further demonstration of Stoppard's abiding claim that politically repressive systems are linguistically repressive also. The problem for the actors is that, like the jumpers, he can do with language what he will. 'I've got the penal code tattooed on my whistle,' he assures Landovsky, 'and there's a lot about you in it.

Section 98, subversion – anyone acting out of hostility to the state . . . Section 100, incitement, anyone acting out of hostility to the state . . . I could nick you just for acting – and the sentence is double for an organised group, which I can make stick on Robinson Crusoe and his man any day of the week' (p. 61). The pun, for the Inspector, is an offensive tactic, a means of making us listen in a certain way: 'You know as well as I do that this performance of yours goes right against the spirit of normalization. When you clean out the stables, Cahoot, the muck is supposed to go into the gutter, not find its way back into the stalls' (p. 62). 'Words,' he announces, happily, 'can be your friend or your enemy, depending on who's throwing the book, so watch your language'(p. 59).

However, the inventiveness of the Inspector is matched, indeed surpassed, by that of the dissidents. Cahoot (who has earlier howled on all-fours and been accused by the Inspector of being in the 'doghouse') starts to abuse him, reminding the audience that 'After-noon, squire,' means, in Dogg, 'Get stuffed, you bastard.' The Inspector asks where Easy learnt Dogg: 'You don't learn it,' replies Cahoot, 'you catch it' (p. 74). This riposte is a triumphant reappli-cation of the formulaic identification of disease with dissent which is at the centre of *Every Good Boy Deserves Favour*, and evidence of Stoppard's appropriation of Wittgenstein's claim that we can learn in a flash. (Compare the Inspector's 'She's making it up as she goes along' (p. 76) when 'Lady Macbeth' starts to translate Shakespeare into Dogg, which is a similar reflection on Wittgenstein – this time on his remarks about the way we evolve rules for new language-games.) The performance of *Macbeth*, and that of Stoppard's own play, now speed to a climax. Dogg becomes a means of repelling the Inspector (his announcement that anything they say will be taken down and played back at the trial meets with the response, 'Bicycles! Plank!' (p. 75)) and of completing *Macbeth* before he realises what is happening. He is at a complete loss as language is wrested from his control. In fact, it is now the Inspector who appears to be spouting nonsense: 'Wilco zebra over,' he bellows into his walkie-talkie, 'Green Charlie Angels 15 out' (p. 76). By teaching his audience Dogg-language Stoppard has implicated them in an act of collective and effective dissent, completing the train of development which successively diminishes the isolation of his characters who criticise the premises and procedures of the Communist state.

In *Dogg's Hamlet, Cahoot's Macbeth*, the jokes, claimed Michael Billington in reviewing the first production, 'are too relentless and by the end the fun has become diagrammatic rather than, in any sense, spontaneous.'[14] The remark reminds us of Stoppard's own praise of Muriel Spark in *Scene*, his claim that, at its best, her work does not so much promulgate a thesis as toy with it, and have fun with it. Although the emphasis on spontaneity is something of a red herring (we have seen how the 'playfulness' of Stoppard's drama is deliberate and pointed rather than simply high-spirited and diverting) Billington has located a problem with *Dogg's Hamlet, Cahoot's Macbeth*. The play protests too much: the slapstick and hectic confusion of the finale are the work of the guilty conscience, abashed by its own earnestness. In *Every Good Boy Deserves Favour, Professional Foul* and *Dogg's Hamlet, Cahoot's Macbeth* Stoppard is on the attack against the iniquities of Communist governments in general, and that of Czechoslovakia in particular. Between the two latter, however, comes *Night and Day* and here, as in *The Real Thing*, his most recent stage play, he is on the defensive: both plays attempt to promulgate a thesis, mounting apologies for the political status quo in Britain. An examination of certain contradictions and confusions in Stoppard's thinking on the relationship of politics and art (and that of drama to the problems it addresses) will prepare the way for an understanding of how *Night and Day* and *The Real Thing* betray his distinctive gifts as a dramatist and how, in the name of freedom, they seek to deny to their audience the possibility of dissent.

7

A Politics of Disengagement

1

The most widespread misapprehension about playwrights (apart from the belief that they have access to unlimited free tickets for their plays), claims Stoppard in an article, 'But For The Middle Classes', 'is that they set out to say something and then say it, in short that the play is the end product of an idea. It is more nearly true to say that the idea is the end product of the play.'[1] He seems to be making here two related points. First, that the dramatist is primarily engaged with the problem of form and, second, that the finished work may, as a consequence, attain a degree of autonomy from its 'author'. 'But For The Middle Classes' is a review of Paul Johnson's book *Enemies of Society* and deserves some detailed attention because it makes explicit Stoppard's feelings about the degree of autonomy his own work has achieved and occupies a central position in his shifting of ideas concerning that relationship between the writer and his work, and between the work and its 'content'.

'Art,' announces *Enemies of Society*, 'is a source not only of pleasure but of reassurance; it is not a luxury of civilisation but a necessity. If art undermines the common attitudes, it lowers morale and makes external assault more deadly.'[2] As a thesis this combines the eccentric and the banal in proportions which Johnson, evidently, does not suspect. His sub-Popperian exercise in socio-historical and art criticism is a restatement of the 'betrayal of the intellectuals'-theme. Modern philosophers and modern artists have, according to Johnson, ranged themselves with those forces undermining man's faith in order, morality and freedom. They represent a threat to the spiritual and social fabric of civilisation. Under the aegis of Wittgenstein and the Cambridge School, Linguistic Philosophy, for instance, has left civilisation undefended by turning away from real problems (such as the determining of man's place in the

123

cosmos) to concentrate on philosophical parlour-games. The philosopher has forsaken his lofty purpose, which Johnson sees as the giving of information about the real world, information which will enable us to orientate ourselves morally. The artist is the philosopher's comrade in treachery, betraying his purpose by wilfully flouting the established rules of realism.

Johnson's argument advances in a series of glides: the only art which gives us the information necessary for our moral-orientation is realistic art, realistic art can only exist in a free society, a society is only genuinely free if economically free. He illustrates his point with the example of Greek sculpture: Greek sculpture is realistic because in Greek society man was free to see himself as he really is. 'The freedom of man in society,' explains Johnson, 'as an economic and political being, was paralleled by the freedom with which the artist could accurately depict him in his optical environment. Only when this freedom was secured by a process of trial, error and improvement, was the information about man complete.'[3] It is a funny sort of free society which is based on slavery, but then, as we shall see, Johnson has a funny sort of idea about freedom.

Johnson's potted history of Western Art assumes that the representational skills of the classical artist are the index of human freedom: he need only identify one to assume the presence of the other. In the last days of the Roman Empire and throughout the Middle Ages man was not free, and so the art was bad: not realistic but symbolic, subordinating the individual to the type. With the early Renaissance, however, things take a turn for the better: painters discover perspective and trade picks up. In other words, the struggles of painters, beginning in the thirteenth century, were a prototype of the economic, social and political struggle in the West to discover a progressive civilisation. Indeed, Giotto's painting inside the Arena Chapel at Padua, 'is one of those rare occasions when we can see civilisation taking off in a cultural sense, rather as it takes off in an economic surge of self-sustaining growth.'[4] The experimental painters of the fourteenth and fifteenth centuries, the technical craftsmen and empirical scientists, as well as the merchants who employed them, were all 'seeking forms of freedom; and their accomplishments were roughly correlated to the degree they secured it. Moreover, all were operating in the middle degree of society and in an urban atmosphere, where the cultural, political and economic limitations on freedom were least oppressive'.[5]

Johnson's misgivings about modern art, however, are perhaps best illustrated by the distinction he draws between Goya's painting, *The Third of May, 1808* and Francis Bacon's series, *The Screaming Pope*. Goya is a man with something to say, and his painting is packed with information: we are given a solid historical context which allows us to relate to it morally. 'Our reactions to this painting may vary greatly,' concedes Johnson, 'but each of us knows where we stand; we are not disorientated. We are given information and draw conclusions.'[6] Bacon, on the other hand, takes as his subject not a real event but just another painting – Velasquez's portrait of Pope Innocent X – and can, as a consequence, tell us nothing worth knowing. Johnson is annoyed with Bacon for not knowing as much about Innocent X as he does (he mentions the 74 year-old's relationship with his widowed sister-in-law, Olympia Maidalchini, and the negligible role he played in the Peace of Westphalia and the end of the Thirty Years' War, to prove his point). In fact, Bacon fails to secure intellectual control over his work and succeeds only in securing the moral disorientation of both himself and his viewer. All we are left with, complains Johnson, is questions: 'Why is the Pope screaming? Who is doing what to him, and why?'[7]

The problem with modern art, insists Johnson, in an unconscious echo of a distinction Stoppard had drawn in *Scene* between writers who tell us little or nothing and those who tell us little or everything, is that it either gives us too little information (as in the case of Bacon, Beckett and Pinter) or (as in the case of Stoppard) too much. Either way, it does not give us the *correct* information and succeeds only in confusing us. Allied to this is art's constant experimentation with form, which is a kind of self-destruction. Art is a huge cultural juggernaut rolling itself and us to spiritual and political disaster as it criticises everything and calls all our certainties into question. We must get back to our classical models, we are warned, or face perdition. Salvation lies in what sounds not unlike State Realism. 'Of course,' Johnson protests, 'the artist is not, and must not be, the servant and defender of an ideology or way of life, as the Soviet authorities (and others) maintain. But neither is he set apart from society; his activities, however motivated, can strengthen or weaken it. Today, it can be argued that the discarding of artistic modes created over centuries contributes precisely to that disorientation of man which we have examined in the previous chapter.'[8] This is all very clumsily done: Johnson combines a declaration of the sanctity of artistic freedom with a heavy-handed reminder that should the artist exercise this freedom he would be radically undermining the fabric of that society which has tolerated his whims. A fetish has been made of freedom: Johnson has identified it totally with a liberal society in which the honest citizen must be allowed to go about his business without a lot of awkward questions being asked by people who should know better, and is incapable of taking a critical look at his own thesis. *Enemies of Society* champions freedom by attempting to curtail it.

In his review of the book Stoppard acknowledges a shared admiration for a Western liberal democracy favouring an intellectual elite and a progressive middle class dedicated to the pursuit of Christian moral values and praises the Popperian influence on Johnson's approach. Proclaiming himself a disciple of Socrates, Karl Popper dates his intellectual maturity from the recognition that, 'any wisdom to which I might ever aspire could consist only in realizing more fully the infinity of my ignorance'.[9] Popper goes on the attack, accordingly, against those systems of thought which claim to have appropriated the whole truth. Johnson, Stoppard notes approvingly, is similarly dismissive of 'closed-circuit systems which explain everything and are irrefutable only in the tactical sense that they avoid the possibility of refutation'.[10] It is, of course, precisely such closed-circuit thinking which Stoppard had exposed in his critique of Logical Positivism in *Jumpers* and would dramatise in the exchanges between the Doctor and Alexander Ivanov in *Every Good Boy Deserves Favour* a few weeks after his article appeared in June 1977. Now he applauds Johnson for continuing Popper's offensive against two powerful proponents of such 'incredible intellectual arrogance': Freudianism and Marxism.

Knowledge, for Popper, is dissent: it is to be approached not through an unquestioning acceptance of dogma, but through the continual criticism and improvement of existing conceptual models. He defines pseudo-scientific thinking as that which devotes itself to the continued verification of a theory. Freudianism and Marxism are pseudo-sciences because they attempt to interpret any conceivable event or phenomenon as verification of their claims. The truly scientific approach is, Popper maintains, to ask as Einstein did, ' "Under what conditions would I admit that my theory is untenable?" In other words, what conceivable facts would I accept as refutations, or falsifications, of my theory?'[11] Scientific thinking (by searching for the edges of our truths, the empirical data which will falsify a theory and lead to the formulation of another) is, then, critical thinking. As such it represents, in Popper's eyes, both a necessary corrective to, and a marked advance upon, the dictates of dogmatism. The critical phase of thinking consists in giving up the dogmatic theory under the pressure of disappointed expectations or refutations. 'But although,' admits Popper, 'the theory of a dogmatic phase followed by a critical phase is too simple, it is true that *there can be no critical phase without a preceding dogmatic phase, a phase in which something – an expectation, a regularity of behaviour – is formed, so that error elimination can begin to work on it.*'[12] Popper's work is an attempt to point out the extent to which Marxism and Freudianism have remained rooted in pseudo-scientific dogma, denying the possibility of all criticism and the formulation of newer, and more serviceable, theories.

Johnson's application of Popper's approach is, Stoppard says, 'a generally compelling display of rational argument and historical reference which is quite capable of disturbing the certainties of at least some of the enemy should it happen to catch them with their minds open'. His praise, however, is substantially qualified on two counts. First, he notes that Johnson is himself prone to the kind of pseudo-scientific statement which, ostensibly, he is attacking. Stoppard feels that his chapter on philosophy is over-selective and over-stressed; by a neat irony, 'his hero Popper is the chief (but not sole) falsification of Johnson's theory that, "because of the strength of the Cambridge philosophical school over the last century, we can fairly say that, if philosophy has failed to be effective and relevant there, it has failed everywhere" '.[13] In espousing Popper's programme for the acquisition of knowledge through criticism, Johnson has failed to criticise his own procedures. He is seizing on all evidence (in the same way as his history of art treats Greek sculpture) with an excess of interpretive zeal.

Second, Stoppard points out that Johnson gets himself into 'deep trouble' when he surveys contemporary art, 'and the reason is his eccentric premise that perspective and illusion (mimesis) is the proper objective of art and a proper criterion by which an artist should be judged'. The implications of Stoppard's strictures are clear and important. Johnson is wrong to dismiss formal innovation. Indeed, by insisting on the enduring superiority of the mimetic approach he lays himself open to the charge of 'formalism' in Sontag's derogatory sense of the term: he is advocating the mechanical perpetuation of outmoded or depleted aesthetic formulae (claiming, for instance, that painting has no real business bothering itself with techniques other than those perfected by Goya). Stoppard also recognises that Johnson's desire to curtail the freedom of the artist in this way entails a concomitant strategy against the audience/viewer. He notes that Johnson finds Bacon pernicious for not answering the questions he raises, but insists that it is 'precisely the unanswered questions which give Bacon's picture the power to make us think beyond the technical expertise of the painter.'[14] We have, in examining his work in *Scene*, already seen Stoppard making this very point: the Chekhovian conviction that the obligation for the artist is the setting rather than the solution of a question, echoed in Beckett's claim that for the artist to answer the question is to clap a snuffer on a candle. In Stoppard's eyes, it is the ability of Bacon's painting to elude comfortable categorisation which allows it to discharge its true responsibilities to the viewer, creating the conditions in which critical activity can be substituted for habitual response.

Stoppard admits that Johnson is generous about his own plays, 'but, more in sorrow than in anger, accuses them of reinforcing the view that reality is an illusion, or at best an uncertain or relative state, and that certitudes are not to be expected in life'. Earlier in the article, Stoppard had described his own repugnance for Marxist Relativism and its claims that facts are not objective but theory-laden: 'These are now the quite familiar teachings of well-educated men and women holding responsible positions in respectable universities, and the thing to say about such teaching is not that it is "radical" but that it is not true. What it is, is false. To claim the contrary is not "interesting". It is silly. Daft. Not very bright. Moreover, it is wicked.' Left to himself, he explains, he subscribes to Johnson's view about what is true and what is false, to objective truth and absolute morality. 'Johnson appears to think that because *Travesties* does not present "real" events in Zürich in 1917, it follows from that that I do not believe in real, truthful history. But I do. My intellect tells me so.' However, he attests to the autonomy of his plays by describing art as not only the child of pure intellect, but equally the child of temperament. This attempt at a quasi-psychological explanation is of less interest than the general point Stoppard is making: the implicit restatement of Wilde's contention that no artist desires to prove anything suggests that the artist is primarily engaged with the problem of form as opposed to 'content'. The chief mistake, he claims, 'is to apply "true or false" criteria to art at all'. Art, as a consequence, 'must be distinguished from other human pursuits which can indeed be true or false, and which deserve to be judged precisely as this book judges them, by the criteria of intellectual truth-statement which do not funk the possibility of refutation'.[15]

Three years previously Stoppard had claimed in *Theatre Quarterly* that art is of fundamental importance, 'because it provides the moral matrix, the moral sensibility from which we make our judgements about the world'.[16] Although, at first sight, this seems to contradict the conclusions we have just seen him reach, it is possible to accommodate this claim to his criticisms of Johnson's model of art's moral function. Johnson claims that Bacon's painting is pernicious because it fails to provide a set of moral co-ordinates (in effect, to inculcate a moral sensibility by invoking a moral law) but his distrust of Bacon's interest in formal innovation is based on what Susan Sontag describes as a fraudulent distinction: the assumed polarity of ethics and aesthetics, the continued plausibility of which rests on our not putting the ethical into question, but only the aesthetic.[17] (Sontag believes Plato responsible for establishing this distinction, so by another neat irony we can see Johnson perpetuating a pseudo-problem caused by one of the enemies of the Open Society condemned so roundly by his hero, Karl Popper.) Sontag says that there is no generic antagonism between the form of consciousness aimed at action, which is morality, and the nourishment of consciousness which is aesthetic experience. Morality, then, is not obedience but free decision based on a genuine apprehension of alternatives and the enemy of morality, no less than of art, is habituation of response. According to this model, Bacon's painting can perform a moral function by offering to the viewer an *aesthetic* experience. Sontag's remarks provide the best way of integrating 'But For The Middle Classes' with Stoppard's earlier description of art as a moral matrix, if we assume that he intends just such an assimilation of ethics to aesthetics – an assimilation which recognises the redundancy, within the work of art, of both intellectual truth-statement (clapping a snuffer on the candle) and of deference to outmoded aesthetic procedures, and which establishes its moral effect as a function of its form.

However, the problem with 'But For The Middle Classes' is not just its uneven tone (the assurance of Stoppard's claims for Bacon contrasts with his rather apologetic defence of his own work) but the fact that it shies away from the implications of this argument. Stoppard does *not* make an explicit assimilation of ethics to aesthetics, instead he allows his case to rest by insisting on the distance between art and those 'other human pursuits' which deserve to be judged as Johnson judges them. Stoppard is trying to have it both ways, to agree with Johnson about the nature of morality *and* to protect art against the consequences. He responds to Johnson's claim that if art undermines the common certitude it lowers morale and makes external assault more deadly, by identifying a confusion between agent and symptom: 'Which are we artists?'[18] If art is merely a symptom of moral uncertainty (as he seems to suggest here) it can hardly be the moral matrix he had claimed it to be in *Theatre Quarterly*. From this angle, 'But For The Middle Classes' looks less like an attempt to counter Johnson's offensive than to sidestep it. The freedom of the artist to produce work which cannot be judged by 'true or false' criteria is preserved, but only by a mystification of process and product; that is to say, Stoppard avoids a thorough or consistent application of the basic premises of his own aesthetics of engagement, an undertaking which would result in a radical questioning of his own, and Johnson's, view of morality.

In this context, Stoppard's claim that 'the idea is the end product of the play' takes on a negative aspect: it allows him to disclaim responsibility for those plays which appear to contradict his conscious beliefs. Yet Stoppard has a long history of making the point (and using the same phrase) in the more positive sense in which it declares that the writer's primary engagement is with form rather than 'content'. 'One writes because one loves writing, really,' he told the *Sunday Times* in 1968; he dismissed the notion that he burned with any causes and said that it was a delusion 'that the play is the end product of an idea; in my experience it is the end product of the play'.[19] Four years later, in 'Playwrights and Professors', he repeated the claim. He described literary criticism ('a pastime fit for educated men of private means and studious bent but no particular talent') as stilted and tautological because founded on 'the mistake which holds literature to be the end product of the ideas it contains, when in truth the ideas are the end product of the literature'.[20] However, perhaps the fullest explication of his view is in a letter to Ken Tynan in which he recalls discussing Logical Positivism with him: 'a sense of renewed endeavour prevails – more concerned with the dramatic possibilities than the ideas, for it is a mistake to assume that plays are the end-products of ideas (which would be limiting): the ideas are the end-products of the plays'.[21] This is clear evidence that, in writing *Jumpers*, Stoppard felt his primary engagement was with the problem of dramatic form rather than 'content'.

Recently, however, Stoppard has taken to denying that these

claims can be taken seriously. He told *Gambit* in 1981 that his early
writing career could best be seen in terms of his sense of alienation
from the Osbornian school of angry young men writing socially-
engaged drama: 'I took on a sort of "travelling pose" which exagger-
ated my insecurity about not being able to fit into this scheme, and
I tended to overcorrect.' However, he had felt the need to change
and had done so in *Jumpers:* 'There the play was the end-product
of an idea as much as the converse.'[22] This appraisal of *Jumpers* not
only contradicts the letter to Tynan, it is itself contradicted by
remarks he had made to Nancy Hardin in 1979. Noting the way his
work presented arguments between conflicting characters (he gives,
as examples, Carr and Tzara, Rosencrantz and Guildenstern, George
and Archie), Stoppard said that 'I tended to write plays which
somehow worked out my own dialogues. But, of course, in a play like
Every Good Boy Deserves Favour the situation is slightly different'.[23]
Here it is the latter play which, in Stoppard's retrospective analysis,
is seen as a decisive break with his earlier work, the play in which,
for the first time (to return to the way he frames the problem in 'But
For The Middle Classes') he sets out to say something, and says it.

It is beyond doubt that Stoppard is conscious of having passed a
watershed in his writing (even if his attempts to locate it are contradictory) and the way he describes this change is important. In *Gambit*
he claims to be preoccupied with simplifying questions and taking
'the sophistication out'. 'A fairly simple question about morality,' he
explains, in an echo of his own Professor Anderson, 'if debated by
highly sophisticated people can lead to almost any conclusion.' To
prove his point he takes the example of the Berlin Wall (and puts
into practice the advice of Chetwyn, who refers moral problems to
his son): 'There's a childlike truth about it. If it was good people
wouldn't want to leave, you wouldn't need to build a wall to keep
them in. "There's something wrong with what you are saying,
Professor!" '. He assures his interviewers that 'in the last few years
I haven't been writing about questions whose answers I believe to be
ambivalent. In *Every Good Boy* and *Professional Foul*, the author's
position isn't ambiguous.'[24] In other words, Stoppard declares
himself concerned with the correct solution, rather than the setting,
of the question. He now positively encourages the application of
'true or false' criteria to his work, thus abandoning the equivocal
position so precariously maintained in 'But For The Middle Classes',
'What Milne says is true. I mean it is true: with a free press everything
is correctible, however imperfect things are they are correctible if

people know they're going on. If we don't know they're going on, it's concealable: true. I believe it to be a true statement. Milne has my prejudice, if you like. Somehow unconsciously, I wanted him to be known to be speaking the truth.'[25] Stoppard now wishes, quite explicitly, not to play with a thesis, but to promulgate it.

The practical consequences of Stoppard's shift can be seen most clearly in his two most recent full-length stage plays. Although he still insists that 'it's nonsense twice over'[26] to suggest that he now burns with a cause and is as concerned as ever to distance himself from 'committed' theatre, the political affiliations of the plays are marked and undeniable. In both the desire to 'take the sophistication' out of questions results in their being presented in such a way as to presuppose their solution; the audience, in other words, is *disengaged* from a set of problems as Stoppard provides the set of moral and political co-ordinates called for in *Enemies of Society*. *The Real Thing* and *Night and Day* show that an aesthetics of engagement has been displaced by a politics of disengagement. *Night and Day* is dedicated to Paul Johnson.

II

Newspaper Drama Is Year's Best New Play ran the joyful headline in the *Daily Telegraph* when *Night and Day* opened at the Phoenix in November 1978. Stoppard had thus won a vociferous new convert in the form of John Barber who applauded both the matter and the manner of the play: the author, he felt, had abandoned the fancy intellectual footwork of his earlier pieces to write 'a savagely serious drama about Fleet Street'. In *The Sunday Times*, however, Bernard Levin was less enamoured. Although he welcomed the 'radically libertarian position' of *Night and Day*, he lamented the opportunity 'most uncharacteristically taken, for some horribly clumsy preaching, stiff with caked earnestness'.[27] He went on to admit to the 'astonishing' realisation that Stoppard had put his viewpoint before his drama, and thus sacrificed the effect of both. This embarrassment of a political ally is perhaps the surest guide to the crudeness of the tactics used by *Night and Day*, tactics which reflect Stoppard's awareness of the politics of literary form.

The setting of *Night and Day* may be Africa but, as Barber notes, its subject is the British press and 'the loyalties a free press inspires'.[28] Stoppard's champion (as he points out in *Gambit*) among the characters holed-up in a luxury bungalow in the middle of an African civil war is Jacob Milne, the young freelance reporter seeking fame and fortune (having fallen foul of union intransigence in Grimsby) who consistently proclaims the importance of a press which is free. For Milne, the only guarantee of a free press is its economic freedom: it must remain the healthy arena for competing entrepreneurial interests. Milne is supported in his views by Ruth, the bored and frustrated wife of his host, who pretends to report the feelings of her son on the subject (following, in a sense, Chetwyn's advice). The general consensus among the Lower Third, she claims, is that freedom is neutral: 'Free expression includes a state of affairs where *any* millionaire can have a national newspaper, if that's what it costs. A state of affairs, Allie says, where only a particular approved, licensed and supervised non-millionaire can have a newspaper is called, for example, Russia.'[29]

Reviewers of the play inevitably found themselves discussing problems close to their hearts and Robert Cushman was not alone in feeling that 'the argument is trivialised'. Michael Billington, for example, raised the objection that Stoppard 'never grapples with the question whether profitability should determine the right to publish opinion or the common-sense fact that the bulk of the English national press supports one particular party'. He might have added that Stoppard does not deal with another commonsense objection: what happens to his free-for-all as the guarantee of press freedom when one of his millionaires, presumably the fittest, wins the struggle and is able to start buying-out his competitors? In the *Spectator* Peter Jenkins voiced his incredulity at the banality of Stoppard's argument: 'I had to keep checking with myself,' he admitted, 'that I wasn't allowing personal hackles to interfere with my judgements that *Night and Day* is a bad play and not a very honest one.'[30]

The problem is Stoppard's unwillingness to take a critical look at his initial premise: that a free-market society is the necessary index of a free one. His argument is simply an extrapolation of the political choice between a society which measures freedom in terms of the individual's putative economic liberties and that which promises economic equality at the expense of other fundamental rights. We are presented with a stark and simple choice, rather than with a problem which might permit of an alternative solution.[31] The two sides of the question do not cancel each other out: they are carefully poised so that criticism of one entails the victory of the other. Ironically, Stoppard also succumbs to the pseudo-scientific thinking he

abhors and which he condemns in 'But For The Middle Classes'.
He interprets all evidence as verification of his thesis, rather than
examining it as a possible refutation: the relative *unanimity* of
political opinion presented in the British national press is seen to
verify the claim that it is the product of a system which encourages
the freedom of expression and the airing of contradictory views.

Milne's principal antagonist is the thick-skinned Australian
journalist, Dick Wagner. As a union man Wagner represents the
stifling pressures of collectivism, while Milne sees himself as a thorn
in the side of union solidarity. 'The *Messenger* isn't officially a closed
shop, you see – ' he says, explaining his metamorphosis into the
Grimsby scab, 'they'd just got used to having a hundred per cent
membership. I gave them a problem' (p. 38). Milne is the Western
version of Stoppard's Soviet dissidents and, as such, is the guardian
of the written and spoken word against appropriation by collective
interests. 'My God,' he cries, accused by Wagner of betraying his
fellow workers, 'you'd need a more supple language than that to
describe an argument between two amoebas' (p. 37). He recalls that
the House Trots at Grimsby spoke ordinary English on subjects like
the death of the novel or the sex life of the editor's secretary, 'but
as soon as they started trying to get me to join the strike it was as
if their brains had been taken out and replaced by one of those little
golf-ball things you get in electric typewriters . . . "Betrayal" . . .
"Confrontation" . . . "Management" . . .' (p. 37). Milne's steward-
ship of ordinary English is continued in his disparaging attack on the
practices of junk-journalism, which 'is the evidence of a society that
has got at least one thing right, that there should be nobody with
the power to dictate where responsible journalism begins' (p. 61).

Significantly, Milne's views on language are justified not only by
the obtuseness of his opponent, they are given tacit support by the
form of *Night and Day* itself. Uncharacteristically for Stoppard, there
are no verbal 'fireworks' in the play. The punning is partial, and it
is Wagner who falls prey to it: lavatory graffiti in Dacca reads, 'Dick
Wagner before he dicks you' (p. 25). Also, the rare passages of
pastiche in *Night and Day* serve to establish a hierarchy of discourse,
not, as in *Travesties*, to cancel one discourse with another. Ruth, for
instance, launches into a parody of travel-brochure clichés about the
tourists' London: she recalls 'Covent Garden porters with baskets of
fruit and veg piled on their heads, threading their way among the
flower girls and the professors of linguistics', and 'The good old
London bobby keeping an eye on the children feeding the beefeaters

outside Buckingham Palace' (p. 43). The parody tricks out Ruth's resentment and frustrated anger, the disillusionment which Milne – the embodiment of positive values – is able to make good. Parodies of house-styles ('Sally Smith is a tea-lady in a Blackpool engineering works, but it was the way she filled those C-cups which got our cameraman all stirred up!' (p. 39)) are enlisted for the same purpose: to justify Milne's claims about the misuse of language, and to establish as privileged his specific viewpoint. The language of *Night and Day*, then, differs from most of Stoppard's previous work in calling attention to itself as theme, not as form. Milne's 'ordinary English' is presented as a 'natural' standard from which all other discourses are deviations.

In effect, Milne is used by Stoppard to proclaim a conservatism which combines the political and the linguistic inasmuch as it declares contrary opinion to be an abuse of *speech*. Similarly the tenacity with which *Night and Day* observes the procedures of Naturalism suggests that a significant departure from them would constitute an abuse of literary form. (Those occasions on which the Naturalistic frame is ruptured are evidence not of a critical concern with formal alternatives, but of a traditional preoccupation with the 'fleshing-out' of character – *vide* those moments in which Ruth voices her unspoken thoughts to the audience.) The binding assumption is of a privileged discourse. What the play presents us with, then, in political, linguistic and literary terms is a 'choice' between sense and nonsense. In effect, *Night and Day* is a closed-circuit, which (like Stoppard's jumpers and his Marxists) attempts to avoid the possibility of refutation.

In a remark recorded by Ken Tynan, Stoppard made Milne's tactic explicitly his own. 'I don't lose any sleep if a policeman in Durham beats somebody up,' he declared, 'because I know it's an exceptional case. It's a sheer perversion of speech to describe the society I live in as one that inflicts violence on the underprivileged. What worries me is not the bourgeois exception but the totalitarian norm. Of all the systems that are on offer, the one I don't want is the one that denies freedom of expression – no matter what its allegedly redeeming virtues may be. The only thing that would make me leave England would be control over free speech.'[32] This articulates succinctly the politics of disengagement defining *Night and Day*. First, it is a retreat from complexity, advocating a perspective in which the 'exceptional case' is reduced in importance. Second, it is a failure of the political and the critical imaginations to engage with real problems (and by presenting a choice between sense and nonsense it seeks to promote a similar failure in its audience). Stoppard refers, significantly, to political systems 'on offer', seeing political commitment as a choice between ready-made alternatives, rather than as their reworking. (This can be contrasted with the way his aesthetics of engagement successfully reworks the alternatives of delinquency and conformity.) It is the same reliance on prefabricated options which prompts Ruth to dismiss too close a scrutiny of the press by pointing first to Fleet Street and then to Russia: the implication being that if you don't have one, you must have the other.

The Real Thing goes a step further than *Night and Day:* dissent from the status quo is regarded not as simply perverse but as fundamentally unreal.

The steward of correct language usage in *The Real Thing* is the playwright Henry who is asked by his wife, Annie, to rework the autobiographical play written by a CND supporter gaoled after an anti-missile rally. 'I know it's raw,' says Annie, 'but he's got something to say.' 'He's got something to say,' comes Henry's response. 'It happens to be something extremely silly and bigoted. But leaving that aside, there is still the problem that he can't write. He can burn things down, but he can't write.'[33] To make his point, Henry brandishes a cricket bat: 'This thing here, which looks like a wooden club, is actually several pieces of particular wood cunningly put together in a certain way so that the whole thing is sprung, like a dance floor.' What Henry is trying to do is 'write cricket bats, so that when you throw up an idea and give it a knock, it might . . . travel.' His objection to Brodie's play is that 'what we've got here is a lump of wood of roughly the same shape trying to be a cricket bat, and if you hit a ball with it, the ball will travel about ten feet and you will drop the bat and dance about shouting "Ouch!" with your hands stuck into your armpits' (p. 53). The difference between the two, Henry insists, is not simply a matter of preference but one of absolute quality: 'This isn't better because someone says it's better, or because there's a conspiracy by the MCC to keep cudgels out of Lords. It's better because it's better' (p. 53).

There are two important and related points here. First, the analogy between the cricket bat and the dramatic artefact provides a crucial contrast with Stoppard's ideas in *Scene.* Although it restates his concern with form and discipline, it also shows that the notion of 'play' has undergone a decisive change: the dramatist now attempts to promulgate 'what he has to say', the idea is knocked in order to *score.* Second, the problem with Brodie's play, according to Henry, is that form and content destroy each other: the rawness of the form, he claims, is inseparable from the inanity of the ideas. Both, in effect, are a perversion of discourse. Henry's cricket bat, in other words, demonstrates not just the necessity of saying things correctly, but of saying the correct things.

Brodie, says Henry, warming to his task, is a 'lout with language'. 'I can't help somebody,' he continues, 'who thinks, or thinks he thinks, that editing a newspaper is censorship, or that throwing bricks is a demonstration while building tower blocks is social violence, or that unpalatable statement is provocation while disrupting the speaker is the exercise of free speech' (p. 55). Brodie's problem is not just that he can't put words together ('traditionally considered advantageous for a writer' (p. 52)); his lack of linguistic facility is inextricably bound up with the nature of his ideas. Brodie does violence upon discourse: 'Words don't deserve that kind of malarkey. They're innocent, neutral, precise, standing for this, describing that, meaning the other, so that if you look after them,' counsels Henry, 'you can build bridges across incomprehension and chaos' (p. 55). The central point is clear: the rawness of Brodie's expression is the index of its untruth. If he really knew how to use the words he does, he could never think the things he thinks he thinks.

Finally, Brodie is dismissed by Henry's appeal to an unquestioned reality which exposes the fraudulence of his ideas. The cricket bat is replaced by the coffee mug as a didactic tool: 'I turn it, and it has no handle. I tilt it, and it has no cavity. But there is something real here which is always a mug with a handle, I suppose' (p. 54). Although prepared to put his trust in the world of objects, Henry will not countenance the reality of politics. 'Public postures,' he had claimed earlier, 'have the configuration of private derangement' (p. 34) and *The Real Thing* moves towards the moment in which Henry's point is proved. The *real* story behind Private Brodie's desecration of the Cenotaph has little enough to do with the siting of nuclear missiles: he was simply out to impress Annie. Annie's work on the Justice for Brodie Committee is likewise exposed: as a political act it has the configuration of her personal atonement of guilt for Brodie's arrest. Snuffer is clapped on candle as she smashes a bowl of dip into Brodie's face. 'You should have told me . . .' suggests Henry, recalling his problems with Brodie's dramatised autobiography. 'That one I would have known how to write' (p. 84).

Political commitment is dismissed as the self that is on offer. The real thing that cancels it, of course, is Henry's love for Annie, and the pain and jealousy he feels when she has an affair with the young actor playing Brodie on television. Michael Billington claims that the play provides 'an unequivocal statement about the joyousness of shared passion', but this is an unduly charitable judgement. Robert Cushman is nearer the mark when he points out that Henry is meant to win through, to rise above jealousy 'and in so doing to prove that his author can create real characters, although people (including, on occasion, himself) have said he can't. If he doesn't bring it off, well, that just proves that the heart's a mystery. It's a double bluff.'[34] What happens is that *The Real Thing* requires precisely that kind of statement identified by Billington as a means of justifying its cancellation of the public and political by the private and the emotional, yet suffers a failure of nerve in the act of making it. In effect, Stoppard launches a pre-emptive strike, criticising Henry's *House of Cards* in terms which might appear equally appropriate to *The Real Thing* itself.

Stoppard ambushes his audience by opening *The Real Thing* with a scene between Charlotte and Max which, it transpires, is taken from *House of Cards*. Later, we hear Charlotte's verdict on the play; what she objects to principally is the polished unreality of Henry's dialogue: 'That's the difference between plays and real life – thinking time, time to get your bottle back.' Henry, she insists, would not sit around being witty like his *alter ego* Max if he caught her out with a lover: 'Like hell he would. He'd come apart like a pick-a-sticks. His sentence structure would go to pot, closely followed by his sphincter' (p. 22). Having established Charlotte's hostile criticism, Stoppard goes on to reflect *The Real Thing* in the mirror of *House of Cards*. The jealous husband of the latter ransacks his wife's belongings while she claims to be in Switzerland and believes he has discovered evidence of her adultery when he finds her passport. Similarly 'theatrical' situations present themselves in *The Real Thing*: Henry's affair with Annie is uncovered by a stained handkerchief and he himself rummages through Annie's things while she is in Glasgow, not quite knowing, perhaps, what he is looking for. Stoppard completes the mirror-image by making his own dialogue a polished reflection of that damned by Charlotte. Henry's idiom is, if anything, more mannered than that of *House of Cards*. A case in point is his declaration, at the height of his confrontation with Annie, that 'We start off like one of those caterpillars designed for a particular leaf. The exclusive voracity of love. And then not. How strange that the way of things is not suspended to meet our special case.' 'I don't want anyone else,' he continues, 'but sometimes, surprisingly, there's someone, not the prettiest or the most available, but you know that in another life it would be her. Or him, don't you find? A small quickening,' he explains, as his sentence structure manifestly does *not* go to pot, in an image combining the mannered with the sentimental to disastrous effect, 'the room responds slightly to being entered. Like a raised blind' (pp. 72–3). Stoppard is trying here to have it both ways. If we do not respond to Henry's effusion as a readily convincing statement of the real thing, we might regard it as a salutary failure of his hyperliterary and self-conscious turn of mind. Stoppard hopes for the first, but will settle for the second. The same is true of Annie's lines at the end of the scene. 'You have to find a part of yourself,' she tells him, 'where I'm not important or you won't be worth loving' (p. 75). In terms of improbably well-turned sententiousness this is not markedly different from 'There's a right thing to say if you can think what it is' (p. 15) – the parallel line from *House of Cards* which Charlotte finds so risible.

In effect, Stoppard is negating the contrast between *House of Cards* and *The Real Thing*. We have seen how Irving Wardle has identified this device as characteristic of what he calls Stoppard's 'looking-glass adventures' in which his mirrors reflect nothing but themselves. In *The Real Thing* the device is the same, but the tactic is different. Stoppard is not establishing different planes of action and then negating the contrast to show each as equally unreal, he is artfully providing himself with a safety-net. The aim is to flatter the audience's belief that it can distinguish between 'good stuff and rubbish' (p. 65) and, simultaneously, to provide an excuse if this qualitative difference fails to declare itself. Stoppard's handling of the comparison between Brodie's rubbish and Henry's rewrite of it is symptomatic. Scene Eleven, when Billy meets Annie on the train, is, it transpires, an excerpt from Henry's television version of Brodie's play (he has earlier ridiculed Brodie's version). In the published text of *The Real Thing* this is made explicit in the final scene when Brodie claims that Henry has been 'clever' with his work: 'I lived it and put my guts into it, and you came along and wrote it clever' (p. 82). What we have been watching, then, is good stuff, the real thing. However, it seems that Stoppard himself had doubts about the quality of his own 'good stuff'. As the scene was performed at the Strand Theatre in November 1982, Billy (playing Brodie) was required to break down, complaining that he could not understand why his character was sitting in a First Class compartment mouthing

first class dialogue. This revision of the published text for performance is characteristic of *The Real Thing:* the play announces itself as
good stuff and, at the same time, acknowledges the suspicion that it
may not be.

Michael Billington claimed that by means of 'fly Pirandellian
games' *The Real Thing* 'questions the nature of reality'.[35] These are
precisely the wrong terms in which to describe the point of the play's
form. In fact, the 'Pirandellian games' perform the same function as
the Naturalism of *Night and Day*. They do not question, they
confirm, demonstrating the real thing, privileged literary discourse.
The play blends its own action with scenes from Strindberg's *Miss
Julie* and Ford's *'Tis Pity She's a Whore*, a door slam recalls *A Doll's
House* and a stained handkerchief *Othello*. In doing so, *The Real
Thing* ranges itself alongside 'fine writing': touchstones of literary
excellence shared by author and audience alike, which help to
measure and confirm the distance between 'good stuff and rubbish'.
Basically, then, the tricksiness of *The Real Thing* is its own point
and the mirror-effect between *House of Cards* and *The Real Thing*
is a vital element of it. Not only does it provide a safety-net for the
play's presentation of emotional realities, it also offers itself as proof
of the play's claim to be 'cunningly put together'. Stoppard parades
the elaborateness which 'places' Brodie's dissent.

Although Henry feels the need to protect language against the
'persuasive nonsense' of his precociously sophisticated sixteen-year-
old daughter (he accuses her of 'Sophistry in a phrase so neat you
can't see the loose end' (p. 68)), the play's formal strategies make
it clear that Stoppard's principal target is not Debbie's dexterity but
Brodie's 'loutish' and restricted way with language, his use of the
cudgel rather than the cricket bat. The form of *The Real Thing* is a
self-conscious demonstration of elaborated discourse and, as such, a
touchstone of the standards violated by Brodie and his ilk. By
opposing its own elaborated form to Brodie's restricted code, the
play draws a sharp line between sense and nonsense (in a tactic
recognisable as that of Stoppard's own jumpers and Marxists) and
puts Brodie firmly on the wrong side of it.

An instructive, and ironic, comparison can be drawn at this point
between *The Real Thing* and Stoppard's 1984 television play about
the Polish Solidarity movement, *Squaring the Circle*. The play is
constructed from a series of disclaimers or denials, Stoppard's point
being that we do not, and cannot, *know* for certain exactly what did
happen in Poland during the months of crisis. The most obvious

instance of such a disclaimer is provided by the two different versions we are given of the meeting in November 1981 of Walesa, Jaruzelski and Archbishop Glemp. In the first version Glemp backs the General, in the second he supports the union leader; the fact that neither version claims to be an objective record of the truth is underlined by the playing-out of the scene as a game of cards.[36] However, the most persistent way that *Squaring the Circle* contradicts itself is by having the Narrator consistently interrupted by a Polish Witness, who denies the version of events we are being given and passes less than flattering comments on the literary quality of the Narrator's efforts. In each instance the Narrator listens to what he is told and bows to superior wisdom. The point is clear: the Narrator's willingness to listen is a corrective to the repressive dogmatism of the Polish authorities. This willingness to listen is in *Squaring the Circle* Stoppard's index of liberalism. (Recounting the tribulations of the Anglo-American production in his introduction to the published text, Stoppard describes his Narrator, ruefully, as 'an unexplained American in Poland' (p. 14)). However, the play also uses the device of disclaimer in a second, and more cunning, way, recognisably similar to the tactics of *The Real Thing*. We are presented on one occasion, for instance, with a powerful visual image: we see a line-up of the Party bosses reviewing a parade – they are dressed as gangsters and talk amongst themselves out of the corners of their mouths. Despite the Narrator's insistence that this is just a metaphor, the Witness protests that it is a distortion and his point is taken (p. 60). The effect is that Stoppard has it both ways: he offers a stereotype, and follows it with a declaration that it is inadequate as a genuine analysis. The example of *The Real Thing* reinforces the suspicion that he hopes we might accept the former, but will settle for our preference for the latter.

The irony of the relationship between the play and the television production is that *The Real Thing* effectively puts the lie to the myth of liberal responsiveness which is the theme and the structural principle of *Squaring the Circle*. The problem with *The Real Thing* is that, in attempting to defend Western Liberal Democracy against its enemies within, Stoppard consigns dissent to nonsense as unequivocally as the Communist authorities in his own plays. *The Real Thing*, no less than *Night and Day*, is precisely that kind of closed-circuit which, in its Marxist forms, Stoppard so abhors. In sealing itself against criticism, Stoppard's work has come to promote a politics of disengagement, which attempts to prevent its audience *engaging* with contrary opinion. In effect, it has hardened into a militant conservatism which, in the way it enlists literary form in its cause, is aesthetic as well as political.

James Saunders has said of his former friend's politics: 'He's basically a displaced person. Therefore, he doesn't want to stick his neck out. He feels grateful to Britain, because he sees himself as a guest here, and that makes it hard for him to criticize Britain. Probably the most damaging thing that could be said about him is that he's made no enemies.'[37] In the light of his more recent work, Saunders' opinion needs to be revised: the most damaging thing that can be said about Stoppard is that in abandoning his aesthetics of engagement he has come to promote a conservative message by adopting tactics he had previously condemned and, in so doing, has put his work at the service of a political thesis which is at best self-contradictory and banal and, at worst, cynical and dishonest.

Notes and References

In all citations London is the place of publication unless otherwise stated. For clarity's sake references to newspaper reviews and articles (and this includes Stoppard's work on *Scene*) will be given in full on each occasion unless a short title is used.

PART I

1. FORMALISM: AN AESTHETICS OF ENGAGEMENT

1. F. Jameson, *The Prison House of Language* (Princeton, 1972) p. 48.
2. L. Trotsky, *Literature and Revolution*, trans. R. Strunsky (New York, 1925) p. 183.
3. See T. Bennett, *Formalism and Marxism* (1979) especially pp. 25–7.
4. S. Sontag, *Against Interpretation* (New York, 1967) p. 27.
5. B. Eichenbaum, 'The Theory of the Formal Method' in L. Matejka and K. Pomorska (eds), *Readings in Russian Poetics* (1971) p. 12.
6. V. Shklovsky, *Mayakovsky and his Circle*, trans. L. Feiler (1974) p. 68.
7. Jameson, *The Prison House of Language*, p. 58.
8. Ibid., pp. 51–2.
9. E. Zola, 'The Experimental Novel and Other Essays' in B. Dukore (ed.), *Dramatic Theory and Criticism: Greeks to Grotowski* (New York, 1974) p. 705.
10. Quoted by Eichenbaum, 'The Theory of the Formal Method', p. 17.
11. Ibid.
12. Quoted by T. Hawkes, *Structuralism and Semiotics* (1977) p. 72.
13. D. Lodge, *Working with Structuralism* (1981) pp. 3–4.
14. Quoted by Eichenbaum, 'The Theory of the Formal Method', p. 31.
15. Jameson, *The Prison House of Language*, p. 64.
16. J. Tynyanov, 'On Literary Evolution' in Matejka and Pomorska (eds), *Readings in Russian Poetics*, p. 74.
17. R. Jakobson, 'The Dominant', ibid., p. 87.
18. B. Brecht, in M. Solomon (ed.), *Marxism and Art* (Brighton, 1979) p. 365.
19. Jameson, *The Prison House of Language*, p. 58.
20. See J. Willett, *Brecht in Context* (1984) pp. 218–21. Willett concludes

that it is the status of Formalism as a politico-aesthetic heresy which has prevented Soviet and East European critics from recognising that Brecht may have derived his key concepts from this source.

21. Quoted by Eichenbaum, 'The Theory of the Formal Method', p. 12.
22. R. Jakobson, 'On Realism in Art' in Matejka and Pomorska (eds), *Readings in Russian Poetics*, p. 40.
23. R. Jakobson and M. Halle, *The Fundamentals of Language* ('S-Gravenhage, 1956) p. 76.
24. Lodge, *Working with Structuralism*, p. 74.
25. Ibid.
26. D. Lodge, *The Modes of Modern Writing* (1977) p. 135.
27. S. Beckett, 'McGreevy on Yeats', *Irish Times* (4 August 1945) 2.
28. S. Beckett, 'Dante . . . Bruno . Vico . . Joyce' in *Our Exagmination Round His Factification for Incamination of Work in Progress* (1972) p. 14.
29. See S. Beckett, 'The Essential and the Incidental', *Bookman* (Christmas 1934) 111.
30. See S. Beckett, 'An Imaginative Work!', *Dublin Magazine* II (July–September 1936) 80.
31. J. Knowlson and J. Pilling, *Frescoes of the Skull* (1979) p. 31.

2. STOPPARD AS CRITIC

1. Interview with M. Amory, *The Sunday Times*, 9 June 1974, 67.
2. Letter to N. Sammells (29 December 1980).
3. R. Bryden, *The Observer*, 28 August 1966, 15; R. Bryden, *The Observer*, 16 April 1967, 24; H. Hobson, *The Sunday Times*, 16 April 1967, 49; P. Hope-Wallace, *Guardian*, 12 April 1967, 7; R. Brustein, *New Republic*, 4 November 1967, 26.
4. Interview with G. Gordon, *Transatlantic Review*, 29 (1968) 23. Stoppard describes his prentice piece *The Gamblers* as highly derivative of Beckett. I have been unable to gain the author's permission to test his claims by examining the unpublished text of the play.
5. *Scene* 7 (25 October 1962) 19.
6. Ibid. 'That sentence,' says Beckett, 'has a wonderful shape. It is the shape that matters.' Interview with H. Hobson, *International Theatre Annual* 1 (1956) 153.
7. First interview in R. Hayman, *Tom Stoppard* (3rd edn, 1979) p. 7.
8. Interview with Gordon, *Transatlantic Review*, 23.
9. *Scene* 7, 19.
10. L. Pirandello, 'On Humour' in B. Dukore (ed.), *Dramatic Theory and Criticism: Greeks to Grotowski* (New York, 1974) p. 750.
11. First interview with Hayman, *Tom Stoppard*, p. 6.
12. *Scene* 6 (19 October 1962) 19.
13. *Scene* 14 (12 December 1962) 44.
14. *Scene* 10 (15 November 1962) 19.
15. Ibid.

16. Interview with D. Gollob and D. Roper, *Gambit* 10 (1981) 12.
17. *Scene* 3 (28 September 1962) 22.
18. Ibid.
19. *Bristol Evening World*, 15 March 1960, 11. Stoppard here anticipates Terry Johnson's *Insignificance* (1982) in which Marilyn Monroe explains the theory of relativity by means of a toy train, a flashlight and a model of Charlie Chaplin.
20. *Bristol Evening World*, 15 March 1960, 11.
21. *Bristol Evening World*, 5 April 1960, 11.
22. Interview with *Theatre Quarterly* 4, 14 (1974) 5.
23. J. W. Lambert, *The Sunday Times*, 31 March 1968, 14; P. Hope-Wallace, *Guardian*, 29 March 1968, 8; I. Wardle, *The Times*, 29 March 1968, 13.
24. *Scene* 14, 44.
25. *Scene* 16 (12 January 1963) 38.
26. *Scene* 20 (9 March 1963) 41.
27. *Scene* 15 (27 December 1962) 30–1.
28. I. Wardle, 'A Grin Without a Cat', *The Times*, 22 June 1968, 19.
29. Quoted by K. Tynan, *Show People* (1980) p. 64.
30. *Scene* 5 (12 December 1962) 4.
31. Ibid., 30.
32. *Rosencrantz and Guildenstern are Dead* (1968) p. 28.
33. *Scene* 5, 30.
34. Quoted in M. Allott (ed.), *Novelists on the Novel* (1959) p.99.
35. S. Beckett, 'Denis Devlin', *transition* 27 (1938) 290.
36. Oscar Wilde, *Plays, Poems and Prose Writings* (1975) p. 69.
37. *Scene* 5, 30.
38. *Scene* 12 (29 November 1962) 19.
39. Interview with J. Watts, *Guardian*, 21 March 1973, 12.
40. *Artist Descending a Staircase & Where Are They Now?* (1973) p. 42.
41. Interview with *Theatre Quarterly*, 6.
42. Letter to N. Sammells (9 April 1981).
43. In R. Rook (ed.), *Play Ten* (1977) p. 4.
44. T. Brassell, *Tom Stoppard: An Assessment* (1985) p. 66.
45. P. Lewis, *Daily Mail*, 24 January 1963, 3; K. Tynan, *The Observer*, 27 January 1963, 24; H. Hobson, *The Sunday Times*, 27 January 1963, 9.
46. W. A. Darlington, *Daily Telegraph*, 24 January 1963, 12; P. Hope-Wallace, *Guardian*, 24 January 1963, 9.
47. J. Saunders, *Next Time I'll Sing To You* (1965) pp. 31–2. All subsequent references will be to this edition and will be incorporated in the text.
48. Tynan, *The Observer*, 27 January 1963, 24.
49. *Scene* 18 (9 February 1963) 6.
50. Ibid., 47.
51. I. Wardle, *The Times*, 18 April 1980, 11.
52. *Scene* 18, 46–7.
53. Interview on Thames Television (28 September 1976). Quoted by Brassell, *Tom Stoppard*, p. 62.

54. Interview with *Theatre Quarterly*, 6.
55. Interview with Amory, 71.
56. Interview with S. Morley, *The Times*, 18 February 1978, 11.
57. See Tynan, *Show People*, p. 71. It is also Tynan who gives the account of the relations between the two men in Berlin.

3. THE NOVEL AS HINGED MIRROR

1. Interview with G. Gordon, *Transatlantic Review*, 29 (1968) 24.
2. See T. Hawkes, *Structuralism and Semiotics* (1977) p. 66 and T. Bennett, *Formalism and Marxism* (1979) p. 23.
3. Quoted by A. Clissmann, *Flann O'Brien* (1975) p. 79.
4. In K. O'Nolan (ed.), *The Best of Myles* (1977) p. 238.
5. F. O'Brien, *At Swim-Two-Birds* (Harmondsworth, 1967) p. 25. All subsequent references will be to this edition.
6. C. Bigsby, *Joe Orton* (1982) p. 15.
7. G. O'Brien, 'Flann O'Brien', *Cambridge Quarterly* 7 (1976–7) 68.
8. *Lord Malquist and Mr Moon* (1980) p. 21.
9. See interview with J. Watts, *Guardian*, 21 March 1973, 12.
10. *Scene* gives an interesting perspective on the closing moments of the novel. Stoppard's review of Athol Fugard's *The Blood Knot* says that 'when the bang comes it is startling to find that the device is one which has been a major inspiration in the plays of Jean Genet, namely that a man will take on the personality of his clothes.' See *Scene* 20 (9 March 1963) 41.

4. A THEATRE OF FORMALISM

1. Quoted by Tynan, *Show People*, p. 47.
2. B. Eichenbaum, 'The Theory of the Formal Method' in Matejka and Pomorska (eds), *Readings in Russian Poetics* (1971) p. 12.
3. See B. Crossley, 'An Investigation of Stoppard's "Hound" and "Foot" ', *Modern Drama* 20 (1977) *passim*.
4. R. Bryden, *The Observer*, 23 June 1968, 26.
5. See M. Billington, *Guardian*, 14 September 1985, 10.
6. *The Real Inspector Hound* (2nd edn, 1970) p. 9.
7. See R. Bryden, *The Observer*, 23 June 1968, 26.
8. Wardle, 'A Grin Without a Cat', 19.
9. Stoppard coins this phrase in a review of Agatha Christie's *Rule of Three*. See *Scene* 16 (12 January 1963) 39.
10. S. Beckett, *Proust* and *Three Dialogues with Georges Duthuit* (1965) p. 23.
11. W. Harris, 'Stoppard's *After Magritte*', *Explicator* 34 (January 1976) *passim*.
12. *Scene* 18, (9 February 1963) 46.

13. *After Magritte* (1971) p. 34.
14. C. James, 'Count Zero Splits the Infinite', *Encounter* 45 (1975) p. 70.
15. K. Hurren, *Spectator*, 12 February 1972, 245; J. Barber, *Daily Telegraph*, 3 February 1972, 11.
16. G. Melly, *The Observer*, 2 July 1967, 19.
17. In *The Dog It Was That Died and Other Plays* (1983) p. 92.
18. 'Paradise and Purgatory', *The Observer Magazine* (29 November 1981) 42.
19. Interview with Gollob and Roper, *Gambit* 10 (1981) 6.
20. *Jumpers* (1972) p. 81.
21. 2nd interview with Hayman, *Tom Stoppard*, p. 143.
22. Interview with F. Hill, *The Times Educational Supplement*, 9 February 1973, 23.
23. F. Marcus, *Sunday Telegraph*, 6 February 1972, 18; J. Barber, *Daily Telegraph*, 3 February 1972, 11.
24. J. Barber, *Daily Telegraph*, 11 June 1974, 14; G. Weales, *Commonweal*, 13 February 1976, 114; J. Elsom, *Listener*, 20 June 1974, 801; Tynan, *Show People*, pp. 113, 119; F. Marcus, *Daily Telegraph*, 16 June 1974, 801; M. Coveney, *Financial Times*, 11 June 1974, 3.
25. G. B. Shaw, 'Preface to Three Plays by Brieux', in B. Dukore (ed.), *Dramatic Theory and Criticism: Greeks to Grotowski* (New York: 1974) p. 636.
26. D. Rod, 'Carr's View on Art and Politics in Tom Stoppard's *Travesties*', *Modern Drama* 26 (1983) 541.
27. Michael Billington, for instance, in reviewing the original London production, suggests that Joyce 'emerges as a truly great man, shaping the way future generations view reality.' (*Guardian*, 11 June 1974, 12.) For a full discussion of the various lobbies for a spokesman in the play, see C. Werner, 'Stoppard's Critical Travesty, or Who Vindicates Whom, and Why . . .', *Arizona Quarterly* 35 (1979) 228–236.
28. Werner, 'Stoppard's Critical Travesty', 230–1.
29. *Travesties* (1975) p. 85.
30. Tynan, *Show People*, p. 109.
31. *Bristol Evening World*, 23 April 1960, 3.
32. Oscar Wilde, *Plays, Poems and Prose Writings* (1975) p. 350. All subsequent references to *The Importance of Being Earnest* and Wilde's critical writings will be to this edition.
33. In the uncut original Wilde allows Algy the most explicit and stylish declaration of this confusion of document and person. Miss Prism expresses the sincere hope that 'you will now turn over a new leaf in life.' 'I have already begun an entire volume, Miss Prism,' comes the reply. See the Four Act version of the play in *The Complete Works of Oscar Wilde* (new edn, 1966) p. 357.
34. For the most succinct discussion of how Stoppard, or Old Carr, cheats history by telescoping four years into one in order to create the events and meetings in *Travesties*, see R. Ellmann, 'The Zealots of Zurich', *The Times Literary Supplement*, 12 July 1974, 744.

35. See G. Lukács, *The Historical Novel*, trans. H. and S. Mitchell (Harmondsworth, 1969) especially pp. 36–39.
36. P. Wood, interview with R. Hayman, *The Times*, 8 June 1974, 9.
37. Quoted by Hayman, *Tom Stoppard*, p. 4. Stoppard is here describing John Hurt's performance in the original production.
38. J. Joyce, *Ulysses* (Harmondsworth, 1969) p. 11.
39. R. Kipling, 'The Elephant's Child', *Just So Stories* (1962) p. 46.
40. H. Zeifman, 'Tomfoolery: Stoppard's Theatrical Puns', *Yearbook of English Studies* 9 (1979) especially 216–18.
41. Tynan, *Show People*, pp. 112–13.

PART II

5. THE DISSENTERS

1. In *Albert's Bridge* and *If You're Glad, I'll be Frank* (1969) p. 45.
2. In *The Dog It Was That Died and Other Plays* (1983) p. 180. This version of the play can be compared with the earlier and slightly fuller version published by French (1977).
3. *Albert's Bridge* (new edn, 1970) pp. 15–16.
4. Fraser's words are a slight variation on those used to describe Moon's feelings. See *Lord Malquist and Mr Moon*, p. 19.
5. S. Mrozek, *Tango*, trans. N. Bethell and T. Stoppard, in M. Esslin (ed.), *Three East European Plays* (Harmondsworth, 1970) p. 114.
6. Ibid., p. 15.
7. J. Bennett, 'Philosophy and Mr Stoppard', *Philosophy* 50 (1975) 5.
8. See A. J. Ayer, *Language, Truth and Logic* (Harmondsworth, 1971) p. 58.
9. B. Russell, *History of Western Philosophy* (2nd edn, 1979) p. 785.
10. Ayer, *Language, Truth and Logic*, p. 142–3.
11. Ibid., p. 157.
12. Bennett, 'Philosophy and Mr Stoppard', p. 6.
13. G. E. Moore, *Principia Ethica* (Cambridge, 1903) p. 17.
14. As W. Hund explains in *The Theory of Goodness in the Writings of G. E. Moore* (Notre Dame, 1964) p. 17, the purpose of Moore's meta-ethics is to show that all ethical meanings refer to the primary meaning of good in a way similar to that in which 'healthy' as predicated of climate, food, medicine, etc., refers to the way it is predicated of an organism.
15. Recalled by A. J. Ayer in *The Central Questions of Philosophy* (Harmondsworth, 1976) p. 38. For a further discussion of Moore's commonsense view of the world, and his taste for practical demonstration to support it, see Ayer's *Russell and Moore: The Analytical Heritage* (1971), especially pp. 175–87. Ayer also discusses here the influence of *Principia Ethica* on the sensibilities of the Bloomsbury Group, p. 137, and the propensity of later linguistic analysts to venerate Moore, rather than Russell. See p. 142 and pp. 244–5.

16. Bennett, 'Philosophy and Mr Stoppard', 6.
17. Ayer, *Language, Truth and Logic*, p. 67.

6. THE DISSIDENTS

1. In *Every Good Boy Deserves Favour and Professional Foul* (1978) p. 56. References to *Every Good Boy Deserves Favour* will also be to this edition.
2. See J. Barber, *Daily Telegraph*, 2 July 1977, 9.
3. B. Levin, *The Sunday Times*, 3 July 1977, 37.
4. M. Billington, *Guardian*, 2 July 1977, 10.
5. Compare *A Separate Peace*, p. 172:
   MATRON   Now, what's your problem, Mr Brown?
   BROWN   I have no problems.
   MATRON   Your complaint.
   BROWN   I have no complaints either. Full marks.
6. Stoppard gives a detailed description of his Moscow trip in 'The Face at the Window', *The Sunday Times*, 27 February 1977, 33.
7. Hayman, *Tom Stoppard*, p. 137.
8. For a discussion of Wittgenstein's early philosophy, see D. Pears, *Wittgenstein* (1971) pp. 45–91.
9. For a discussion of the importance of Wittgenstein's emphasis in the 'Tractatus' on the misleading nature of ordinary language, see J. Urmson, *Philosophical Analysis* (Oxford, 1956), especially pp. 102–7.
10. L. Wittgenstein, *Philosophical Investigations*, trans G. Anscombe (Oxford, 2nd edn, 1958), point 23.
11. Ibid., point 83.
12. Ibid., point 197.
13. *Dogg's Hamlet, Cahoot's Macbeth* (1980) p. 58.
14. M. Billington, *Guardian*, 17 July 1979, 8.

7. A POLITICS OF DISENGAGEMENT

1. 'But For The Middle Classes', *The Times Literary Supplement*, 3 June 1977, 677.
2. P. Johnson, *Enemies of Society* (1977) p. 226.
3. Ibid., pp. 43–4.
4. Ibid., p. 48.
5. Ibid., p. 51.
6. Ibid., p. 222.
7. Ibid., p. 223.
8. Ibid., p. 214.
9. K. Popper, *Unended Quest* (1976) p. 7.
10. 'But For The Middle Classes', 677.
11. Popper, *Unended Quest*, p. 41.

12. Ibid., p. 51.
13. 'But For The Middle Classes', 677.
14. Ibid.
15. Ibid.
16. Interview with *Theatre Quarterly*, 4 (1974) 14.
17. Sontag, *Against Interpretation* (New York, 1967) p. 23.
18. 'But For The Middle Classes', 677.
19. 'Something to Declare', *The Sunday Times*, 25 February 1968, 47.
20. 'Playwrights and Professors', *The Times Literary Supplement*, 13 October 1972, 1219.
21. Quoted by Tynan, *Show People*, p. 91.
22. Interview with Gollob and Roper, *Gambit* 10 (1981) 6.
23. Interview with N. Hardin, *Contemporary Literature*, 22 (1981) 158.
24. Interview with Gollob and Roper, 17.
25. Ibid., 15.
26. Interview with Hardin, 52.
27. J. Barber, *Daily Telegraph*, 9 November 1978, 15; B. Levin, *The Sunday Times*, 12 November 1978, 37.
28. J. Barber, *Daily Telegraph*, 9 November 1978, 15.
29. *Night and Day* (2nd edn, 1979) p. 84.
30. R. Cushman, *The Observer*, 12 November 1978, 33; M. Billington, *Guardian*, 9 November 1978, 12; P. Jenkins, *Spectator*, 18 November 1978, 24.
31. The argument looks, indeed, like a bad case of 'Cold War Calvinism' which, according to E. P. Thompson, 'commences within the premises of the Cold War and assumes that no other premises are possible. It is predicated upon that facile division of the world into binary antinomies which has so often tricked the human mind: good/bad, the damned and the saved.' See *Guardian*, 31 August 1981, 10.
32. Quoted by Tynan, *Show People*, p. 100.
33. *The Real Thing* (1983) p. 50.
34. M. Billington, *Guardian*, 17 November 1982, 9; R. Cushman, *The Observer*, 21 November 1982, 30.
35. M. Billington, *Guardian*, 17 November 1982, 9.
36. *Squaring the Circle* (1984) pp. 88–91.
37. Tynan, *Show People*, p. 71.

Bibliography

1. GENERAL (SELECT)

This section lists only those books cited directly in the text or notes.

Allott, M. (ed.), *Novelists on the Novel* (London: Routledge & Kegan Paul, 1959).

Ayer, A. J., *Language, Truth and Logic* (Harmondsworth: Penguin, 1971).

——————, *Russell and Moore: The Analytical Heritage* (London: Macmillan, 1971).

——————, *The Central Questions of Philosophy* (Harmondsworth: Penguin, 1976).

Beckett, S., *Proust* and *Three Dialogues with Georges Duthuit* (London: Calder, 1965).

——————*et al., Our Exagmination Round His Factification for Incamination of Work in Progress* (London: Faber, 1972).

Bennett, T., *Formalism and Marxism* (London: Methuen, 1979).

Bigsby, C., *Joe Orton* (London: Methuen, 1982).

Clissmann, A., *Flann O'Brien* (London: Macmillan, 1975).

Dukore, B. (ed.), *Dramatic Theory and Criticism: Greeks to Grotowski* (New York: Holt, Rinehart & Winston, 1974).

Hawkes, T., *Structuralism and Semiotics* (London: Methuen, 1977).

Hund, W., *The Theory of Goodness in the Writings of G. E. Moore* (Notre Dame: [Dissertation], 1964).

Jakobson, R. and Halle, M., *The Fundamentals of Language* ('S-Gravenhage: Mouton, 1956).

Jameson, F., *The Prison House of Language* (Princeton: Princeton University Press, 1972).

Johnson, P., *Enemies of Society* (London: Weidenfeld & Nicolson, 1977).

Johnson, T., *Insignificance* (London: Methuen, 1982).

Joyce, J., *Ulysses* (Harmondsworth: Penguin, 1969).

Kipling, R., *Just So Stories* (London: Macmillan, 1962).

Knowlson, J. and Pilling, J., *Frescoes of the Skull: The Later Prose and Drama of Samuel Beckett* (London: Calder, 1979).

Lodge, D., *The Modes of Modern Writing* (London: Edward Arnold, 1977).

——————, *Working with Structuralism* (London: Routledge & Kegan Paul, 1981).

Lukács, G., *The Historical Novel*, translated by H. and S. Mitchell (Harmondsworth: Penguin, 1969).

Matejka, L. and Pomorska, K. (eds), *Readings in Russian Poetics*. (London: MIT Press, 1971).

Moore, G. E., *Principia Ethica* (Cambridge: Cambridge University Press, 1903).

O'Brien, F., *At Swim-Two-Birds* (Harmondsworth: Penguin Books, 1967).

————, [Myles NaGopaleen], *The Best of Myles*, ed. K. O'Nolan (London: Picador, 1977).

Pears, D., *Wittgenstein* (London: Fontana, 1971).

Popper, K., *Unended Quest* (London: Fontana, 1976).

Rook, R. (ed.), *Play Ten* (London: Edward Arnold, 1977).

Russell, B., *History of Western Philosophy*, 2nd edn (London: Allen & Unwin, 1979).

Saunders, J., *Next Time I'll Sing To You* (London: Heinemann, 1965).

Shklovsky, V., *Mayakovsky and his Circle*, trans. L. Feiler (London: Pluto Press, 1974).

Solomon, M. (ed.), *Marxism and Art* (Brighton: Harvester Press, 1979).

Sontag, S., *Against Interpretation* (New York: Farrar, Strauss & Giroux, 1967).

Trotsky, L., *Literature and Revolution*, trans. R. Strunsky (New York: International Publishers, 1925).

Urmson, J., *Philosophical Analysis* (Oxford: Oxford University Press, 1956).

Wilde, O., *The Complete Works of Oscar Wilde*, new edn (London: Collins, 1966).

————, *Plays, Poems and Prose Writings* (London: Dent & Dutton, 1975).

Willett, J., *Brecht in Context* (London: Methuen, 1984).

Wittgenstein, L., *Philosophical Investigations*, trans. G. Anscombe, 2nd edn (Oxford: Oxford University Press, 1958).

2. STOPPARD: WORKS

(*Second and new editions are listed only if they are cited in the text.*)

After Magritte (London: Faber, 1971).

Albert's Bridge, new edn (London: Faber, 1970).

Albert's Bridge and *If You're Glad, I'll be Frank* (London: Faber, 1969).

Artist Descending a Staircase and *Where Are They Now?* (London: Faber, 1973).

Dirty Linen and *New-Found-Land* (London: Faber, 1976).

The Dog It Was That Died and Other Plays [*The Dissolution of Dominic Boot*, '*M' is for Moon Among Other Things, Teeth, Another Moon Called Earth, Neutral Ground, A Separate Peace*] (London: Faber, 1983).

Dogg's Hamlet, Cahoot's Macbeth (London: Faber, 1980).

Dogg's Our Pet and *The (15-Minute) Dogg's Troupe Hamlet*, in E. Berman (ed.), *Ten of the Best British Short Plays* (London: Inter-Action Imprint, 1979).

Enter a Free Man (London: Faber, 1968).

Every Good Boy Deserves Favour and *Professional Foul* (London: Faber, 1978).

The 15-Minute Hamlet (London: French, 1976).

Four Plays for Radio [*Artist Descending a Staircase, Where Are They Now?,
If You're Glad, I'll be Frank, Albert's Bridge*] (London: Faber, 1984).
Jumpers (London: Faber, 1972).
Lord Malquist and Mr Moon (London: Faber, 1980).
Night and Day, 2nd edn (London: Faber, 1979).
The Real Inspector Hound, 2nd edn (London: Faber, 1970).
The Real Thing (London: Faber, 1983).
'Reunion', 'Life, Times: Fragments', 'The Story' in *Introduction 2* (London:
Faber, 1960).
Rosencrantz and Guildenstern are Dead (London: Faber, 1968).
A Separate Peace (London: French, 1977).
Squaring the Circle (London: Faber, 1984).
Travesties (London: Faber, 1975).

Adaptations

Dalliance and *Undiscovered Country*, adapted from A. Schnitzler (London:
Faber, 1986).
On The Razzle, adapted from J. Nestroy (London: Faber, 1981).
Rough Crossing, adapted from F. Molnár (London: Faber, 1985).
Tango, with N. Bethell, adapted from S. Mrozek, in M. Esslin (ed.), *Three
East European Plays* (Harmondsworth: Penguin, 1970).
Undiscovered Country, adapted from A. Schnitzler (London: Faber, 1980).

3. STOPPARD: OCCASIONAL ARTICLES

'Something to Declare', *The Sunday Times*, 25 February 1968, 25.
'Orghast' [Review], *The Times Literary Supplement*, 1 October 1971, 1174.
'Yes, We Have No Banana', *Guardian*, 10 December 1971, 10.
'Playwrights and Professors', *The Times Literary Supplement*, 13 October
1972, 1219.
'Dirty Linen in Prague', *New York Times*, 11 February 1977, 27.
'The Face at the Window', *The Sunday Times*, 27 February 1977, 33.
'But For The Middle Classes', *The Times Literary Supplement*, 3 June 1977,
677.
'Prague: The Story of the Chartists', *New York Review of Books*, 4 August
1977, 11–15.
'KGB's Olympic Trials', *The Sunday Times*, 6 April 1980, 16.
'Paradise and Purgatory', *The Observer Magazine*, 29 November 1981,
38–50.

4. BOOKS ON STOPPARD

Bigsby, C., *Tom Stoppard* (Harlow: Longman for the British Council, 1976).
Brassell, T., *Tom Stoppard: An Assessment* (London: Macmillan, 1985).

Cahn, V., *Beyond Absurdity* (London: Associated Universities Press, 1979).
Corballis, R., *Tom Stoppard: The Mystery and the Clockwork* (London: Methuen, 1984).
Dean, J., *Tom Stoppard: Comedy as a Moral Matrix* (Columbia: University of Missouri Press, 1981).
Hayman, R., *Tom Stoppard*, 3rd edn (London: Heinemann, 1979).
Hunter, J., *Tom Stoppard's Plays* (London: Faber, 1982).
Whitaker, T., *Tom Stoppard* (London: Macmillan, 1983).

5. BOOKS PARTIALLY DEVOTED TO STOPPARD

Cohn, R., *Modern Shakespeare Offshoots* (Guildford: Princeton University Press, 1976) pp. 211–18.
Colby, D., *As The Curtain Rises* (Rutherford: Farleigh Dickinson University Press, 1978) pp. 29–45.
Gardner, J., *On Moral Fiction* (New York: Basic Books, 1978) pp. 58–9.
Gaskell, P., *From Writer to Reader: Studies in Editorial Method* (Oxford: Clarendon Press, 1978) pp. 245–62.
Hayman, R., *Theatre and Anti-Theatre: New Movements since Beckett* (London: Secker & Warburg, 1979) pp. 138–46.
Kerensky, O., *The New British Drama: Fourteen Playwrights since Osborne and Pinter* (London: Hamilton, 1977) pp. 145–71.
Marowitz, C., *Confessions of a Counterfeit Critic: A London Theatre Note-book, 1958–71* (London: Eyre Methuen, 1973) pp. 123–6.
Schlueter, J., *Metafictional Characters in Modern Drama* (Guildford: Columbia University Press, 1979) pp. 89–103.
Schwartz, A., *From Büchner to Beckett: Dramatic Theory and the Modes of Tragic Drama* (Athens: Ohio University Press, 1978) pp. 326–32.
Taylor, J., *Anger and After*, 2nd edn (London: Methuen, 1969) pp. 318–20.
————, *The Second Wave: British Drama for the Seventies* (London: Methuen, 1971) pp. 94–107.
Tynan, K., *Show People* (London: Weidenfeld & Nicolson, 1980) pp. 44–123.

6. ARTICLES ON STOPPARD

Asmus, W., '*Rosencrantz and Guildenstern are Dead*', *Shakespeare-Jahrbuch*, 106 (1970) 118–31.
Ayer, A. J., 'Love Among the Logical Positivists', *The Sunday Times*, 9 April 1974, 16.
Babula, W., 'The Play-Life Metaphor in Shakespeare and Stoppard', *Modern Drama*, 15 (1972) 279–81.
Barber, J., 'Tom Stoppard at a Terminus', *Daily Telegraph*, 4 July 1977, 10.
Bennett, J., 'Philosophy and Mr Stoppard', *Philosophy*, 50 (1975) 5–18.

Berlin, N., *'Rosencrantz and Guildenstern are Dead:* Theatre of Criticism', *Modern Drama*, 16 (1973) 269–77.

Billman, C., 'The Art of History in Tom Stoppard's *Travesties'*, *Kansas Quarterly*, 12 (1980) 47–52.

Brassell, T., *'Jumpers:* A Happy Marriage', *Gambit*, 10 (1981) 43–59.

Buhr, R., 'Epistemology and Ethics in Tom Stoppard's *Professional Foul'*, *Comparative Drama*, 13 (1979) 320–29.

————, 'The Philosophy Game in Tom Stoppard's *Professional Foul'*, *Midwest Quarterly*, 22 (1980–81) 407–15.

Callen, A., 'Stoppard's Godot: Some French Influences on Post-War English Drama', *New Theatre Magazine*, 10 (1969) 22–30.

Camroux, D., 'Tom Stoppard: The Last of the Metaphysical Egocentrics', *Caliban*, 15 (1978) 79–94.

Cohn, R., 'Tom Stoppard: Light Drama and Dirges in Marriage', in C. Bigsby (ed.), *Contemporary English Theatre: Stratford-Upon-Avon Studies*, 19 (London: Edward Arnold, 1981) pp. 109–20.

Cooke, J., 'The Optical Allusion: Repetition and Form in Stoppard's *Travesties'*, *Modern Drama*, 24 (1981) 523–39.

Corballis, R. 'Extending the Audience: The Structure of *Rosencrantz and Guildenstern are Dead'*, *Ariel*, 11 (1980) 65–79.

Crick, B., *'Travesties'*, *The Times Higher Educational Supplement*, 2 August 1974, 13.

Crossley, B., 'An Investigation of Stoppard's "Hound" and "Foot" ', *Modern Drama*, 20 (1977) 77–86.

Crump, G., 'The Universe as Murder Mystery: Tom Stoppard's *Jumpers'*, *Comparative Drama*, 20 (1979) 354–68.

Davidson, M., 'Historical Homonyms: A New Way of Naming in *Jumpers'*, *Modern Drama*, 22 (1979) 305–13.

————, 'Transcending Logic: Stoppard, Wittgenstein, and Aristophanes', in K. White (ed.), *Alogical Modern Drama* (Amsterdam: Rodopi, 1982).

Delaney, P., 'The Flesh and the Word in *Jumpers'*, *Modern Language Quarterly*, 42 (1981) 369–88.

————, 'Cricket Bats and Commitment: The Real Thing in Art and Life', *Critical Quarterly*, 27 (1985) 45–60.

Dobrin, D., 'Stoppard's *Travesties'*, *Explicator*, 40 (1981) 63–4.

Duncan, J., 'Godot Comes: *Rosencrantz and Guildenstern are Dead'*, *Ariel*, 12 (1981) 57–70.

Egan, R., 'A Thin Beam of Light: The Purpose of Playing in *Rosencrantz and Guildenstern are Dead'*, *Educational Theatre Journal*, 31 (1979) 59–69.

Elam, K., 'After Magritte, after Carroll, after Wittgenstein: What Tom Stoppard's Tortoise Taught Us', *Modern Drama*, 27 (1984) 469–85.

Ellmann, R., 'The Zealots of Zurich', *The Times Literary Supplement*, 12 July 1974, 744.

Gabbard, L., *'Jumpers:* A Murder Mystery', *Modern Drama*, 20 (1977) 87–95.

Gitzen, J., 'Tom Stoppard: Chaos in Perspective', *Southern Humanities Review*, 10 (1976) 143–52.

Gold, M., 'Who are the Dadas of *Travesties?*' *Modern Drama*, 21 (1978) 59–65.

Gruber, W., ' "Wheels within Wheels, etc.," Artistic Design in *Rosencrantz and Guildenstern are Dead*', *Comparative Drama*, 15 (1981–2) 291–310.

Harris, W., 'Stoppard's *After Magritte*', *Explicator*, 34 (January 1976) item 40.

Hinden, M., '*Jumpers:* Stoppard and the Theatre of Exhaustion', *Twentieth Century Literature*, 27 (1981) 1–5.

Holubetz, M., 'A Mockery of Theatrical Conventions: The Fake Death Scenes in *The White Devil* and *Rosencrantz and Guildenstern are Dead*', *English Studies*, 63 (1982) 426–29.

James, C., 'Count Zero Splits the Infinite', *Encounter*, 45 (1975) 68–76.

Kennedy, A., 'Old and New in London Now', *Modern Drama*, 11 (1968–9), 437–46.

————, 'Natural, Mannered and Parodic Dialogue', *Yearbook of English Studies*, 9 (1979) 28–54.

————, 'Tom Stoppard's Dissident Comedies', *Modern Drama*, 25 (1982) 469–76.

Keyssar-Franke, H., 'The Strategy of *Rosencrantz and Guildenstern are Dead*', *Educational Theatre Journal*, 27 (1975) 85–97.

Lee, R., 'The Circle and its Tangent', *Theoria*, 33 (1969) 37–43.

Levenson, J., 'Views from a Revolving Door: Stoppard's Canon to Date', *Queen's Quarterly*, 78 (1971) 431–42.

————, '*Hamlet* andante/*Hamlet* allegro: Tom Stoppard's two versions', *Shakespeare Survey*, 36 (1983) 21–8.

Levy, B., 'Serious Propositions Compromised by Frivolity', *Critical Quarterly*, 22 (1980) 79–85.

McMillan, D., 'Dropping the Other Boot', *Gambit*, 10 (1981) 61–76.

Marowitz, C., 'Tom Stoppard: The Theatre's Intellectual P. T. Barnum', *New York Times*, 19 October 1975, Section 2, 5.

Morwood, J., '*Jumpers* Revisited', *Agenda*, 18 (1981) 135–41.

Novick, J., 'Going Plume on Plume', *Village Voice*, 31 January 1977, 69.

Pearce, H., 'Stage as Mirror: Tom Stoppard's *Travesties*', *Modern Language Notes*, 94 (1979) 1139–58.

Rabinowitz, P., 'What's Hecuba to Us?: The Audience's Experience of Literary Borrowing', in S. Suleiman and I. Crosman (eds), *The Reader and the Text* (Princeton: Princeton University Press, 1980) pp. 241–63.

Roberts, P.,.'Tom Stoppard: Serious Artist or Siren?' *Critical Quarterly*, 20 (1978) 84–92.

Robinson, G., 'Plays without Plot: The Theatre of Tom Stoppard', *English Theatre Studies*, 29 (1977) 37–48.

Rod, D., 'Carr's Views on Art and Politics in Tom Stoppard's *Travesties*', *Modern Drama*, 26 (1983) 536–42.

Rodway, A., 'Stripping Off', *London Magazine*, 16 (1976) 65.

Rothstein, B., 'The Reappearance of Public Man: Tom Stoppard's *Jumpers* and *Professional Foul*', *Kansas Quarterly*, 12 (1980) 35–46.

Ruskin, P. and Lutterbie, J., 'Balancing the Equation', *Modern Drama*, 26 (1983) 543–45.

Salmon, E., 'Faith in Tom Stoppard', *Queen's Quarterly*, 86 (1979) 215–32.

Sammells, N., 'Tom Stoppard and the Politics of Listening', in G. MacGregor and R. S. White (eds), *The Art of Listening* (London: Croom Helm, 1986) pp. 179–200.

————, 'The Aniseed Trail and the Metaphysical Fox: Tom Stoppard's *Jumpers*', *Swansea Review*, 1 (1986) 46–56.

Schwartzmann, M., 'Wilde about Joyce: Stoppard's *Travesties*', *James Joyce Quarterly*, 13 (1975) 122–3.

Scruton, R., 'The Real Stoppard', *Encounter*, 60 (1983) 44–7.

Shiner, R., 'Showing, Saying and Jumping', *Dialogue*, 21 (1982) 625–46.

Simard, R., 'The Logic of Unicorns: Beyond Absurdism in Stoppard', *Arizona Quarterly*, 38 (1982) 37–44.

Simons, J., '*Night and Day*', *Gambit*, 10 (1981) 77–85.

Varey, S., 'Nobody Special: *Rosencrantz and Guildenstern are Dead*', *Dutch Quarterly Review*,10 (1980) 20–31.

Wardle, I., 'A Grin Without a Cat', *The Times*, 22 June 1968, 19.

Weightman, J., '*Jumpers:* a Metaphysical Comedy', *Encounter*, 38 (1972) 44–6.

Werner, C., 'Stoppard's Critical Travesty, or Who Vindicates Whom, and Why . . .' *Arizona Quarterly*, 35 (1979) 228–36.

Whitaker, T., 'Notes on Playing the Player', *Centennial Review*, 16 (1972) 1–2.

Wilcher, R., 'The Museum of Tragedy: *Endgame* and *Rosencrantz and Guildenstern are Dead*', *Journal of Beckett Studies*, 4 (1979) 43–54.

Zeifman, H., 'Tomfoolery: Stoppard's Theatrical Puns', *Yearbook of English Studies*, 9 (1979) 204–20.

————, 'Comedy of Ambush: Tom Stoppard's *The Real Thing*', *Modern Drama*, 26 (1983) 139–49.

7. INTERVIEWS AND PROFILES

(When no author is given the entry is alphabetised either by title or periodical, to make reference from notes easier.)

Amory, M., *The Sunday Times Magazine*, 9 June 1974, 64–71.

Connolly, R., *The Sunday Times*, 20 January 1980, 32.

Cook, B., *The Saturday Review*, 8 January 1977, 52–3.

Dutch Quarterly Review, 10 (1980) 41–57.

Gollob, D., and Roper, D., *Gambit*, 10 (1981) 5–17.

Gordon, G., *Transatlantic Review*, 29 (1968) 17–25.

Halton, K., *Vogue*, 15 October 1967, 112.

Hardin, N., *Contemporary Literature*, 22 (1981) 153–66.

Harper, K., *Guardian*, 12 April 1967, 7.

Hayman, R., *The Sunday Times Magazine*, 2 March 1980, 29–33.

Hill, F., *The Times Educational Supplement*, 9 February 1973, 23.

'I'm Not Keen on Experiments', *New York Times*, 8 March 1970, Section 2, 17.

'*Jumpers* Author is Verbal Gymnast', *New York Times*, 23 April 1974, 36.

Kroll, J., *Newsweek*, 16 January 1984, 49–50.

May, C., and Behr, E., *Newsweek*, 15 August 1977, 35–40.
Norman, B., *The Times*, 11 November 1972, 30.
Popkin, H., *The Sunday Times*, 17 February 1980, 41.
Theatre Quarterly 4, 14 (1974) 3–17.
Watts, J., *Guardian*, 21 March 1973, 12.
'Writing's My 43rd Priority', *The Observer*, 17 December 1967, 4.

8. TELEVISION INTERVIEWS AND FEATURES

(listed chronologically)
7 July 1972, *BBC 1* [*One Pair of Eyes*]
28 September 1976, *ITV* [*The South Bank Show*]
22 April 1983, *ITV* [*Writers on Writing*]
17 October 1983, *BBC 2* [Interview with Frank Delaney]

Index

159